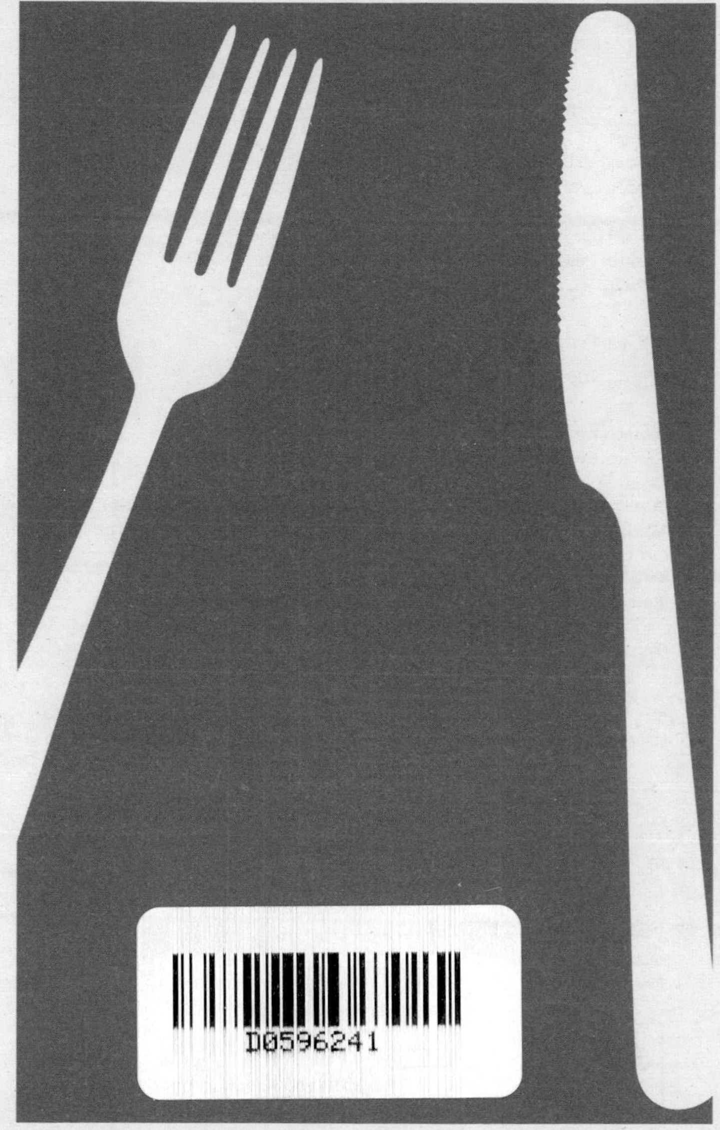

1 3 5 7 9 10 8 6 4 2

Vintage
20 Vauxhall Bridge Road,
London SW1V 2SA

Vintage Classics is part of the Penguin Random House group of companies whose addresses can be found at global.penguinrandomhouse.com.

How To Eat was first published in Great Britain by Chatto & Windus in 1998
Kitchen was first published in Great Britain by Chatto & Windus in 2010

This edition published by Vintage in 2017

www.vintage-books.co.uk

A CIP catalogue record for this book is available from the British Library

ISBN 9781784872656

Typeset in 9.5/14.5 pt FreightText Pro
by Jouve (UK), Milton Keynes
Printed and bound by Clays Ltd, St Ives plc

Penguin Random House is committed to a sustainable future for our business, our readers and our planet. This book is made from Forest Stewardship Council® certified paper.

Eating

NIGELLA LAWSON

VINTAGE MINIS

Contents

Preface

Cooking is not about just joining the dots, following one recipe slavishly and then moving on to the next. It's about developing an understanding of food, a sense of assurance in the kitchen, about the simple desire to make yourself something to eat. And in cooking, as in writing, you must please yourself to please others. Strangely it can take enormous confidence to trust your own palate, follow your own instincts. Without habit, which itself is just trial and error, this can be harder than following the most elaborate of recipes. But it's what works, what's important.

There is a reason why this volume is called Eating rather than Cooking. It's a simple one: although it's possible to love eating without being able to cook, I don't believe you can ever really cook unless you love eating. Such love, of course, is not something which can be taught, but it can be conveyed – and maybe that's the point. In writing this book, I wanted to make food and my slavering passion for it the starting point; indeed for me it *was* the starting point. I have nothing to declare but my greed.

The French, who've lost something of their culinary confidence in recent years, remain solid on this front. Some years ago in France, in response to the gastronomic apathy and consequent lowering of standards nationally – what is known as *la crise* – Jack Lang, then Minister of Culture, initiated *la semaine du goût*. He set up a body expressly to go into schools and other institutions not to teach anyone how to cook, but how to eat. This group might take with it a perfect baguette, an exquisite cheese, some local speciality cooked *comme il faut*, some fruit and vegetables grown properly and picked when ripe, in the belief that if the pupils, if people generally, tasted what was good, what was right, they would respect these traditions; by eating good food, they would want to cook it. And so the cycle continues.

I suppose you could say that we, over here, have had our own unofficial version of this. Our gastronomic awakening – or however, and with whatever degree of irony, you want to describe it – has been to a huge extent restaurant-led. It is, you might argue, by tasting food that we have become interested in cooking it. I do not necessarily disparage the influence of the restaurant: I spent twelve years as a restaurant critic, after all. But restaurant food and home food are not the same thing. Or, more accurately, eating in restaurants is not the same thing as eating at home. Which is not to say, of course, that you can't borrow from restaurant menus and adapt their chefs' recipes – and I do. This leads me to the other reason this book is about How to Eat.

I am not a chef. I am not even a trained or professional cook. My qualification is as an eater. I cook what I want to eat – within limits. I have a job – another job, that is, as an ordinary working journalist – and two children, one of whom was born during the writing of this book. And during the book's gestation, I would sometimes plan to cook some wonderful something or other, then work out a recipe, apply myself in anticipatory fantasy to it, write out the shopping list, plan the dinner – and then find that when it came down to it I just didn't have the energy. Anything that was too hard, too fiddly, filled me with dread and panic or, even if attempted, didn't work or was unreasonably demanding, has not found its way in here. And the recipes I do include have all been cooked in what television people call Real Time: menus have been made with all their component parts, together; that way, I know whether the oven settings correspond, whether you'll have enough hob space, how to make the timings work and how not to have a nervous breakdown about it. I wanted food that can be made and eaten in a real life, not in perfect, isolated laboratory conditions.

Much of this is touched upon throughout the book, but I want to make it clear, here and now, that you need to acquire your own individual sense of what food is about, rather than just a vast collection of recipes.

What I am not talking about, however, is strenuous originality. The innovative in cooking all too often turns out to be inedible. The great Modernist dictum, Make It New, is not a helpful precept in the kitchen. 'Too often,' wrote the great society hostess and arch foodwriter Ruth Lowinsky, as early as 1935, 'the inexperienced think that if food is odd it must be a success. An indifferently roasted leg of mutton is not transformed by a sauce of hot raspberry jam, nor a plate of watery consommé improved by the addition of three glacé cherries.' With food, authenticity is not the same thing as originality; indeed they are often at odds. So while much is my own here – insofar as anything can be – many of the recipes included are derived from other writers. From the outset I wanted this book to be, in part, an anthology of the food I love eating and a way of paying my respects to the foodwriters I've loved reading. Throughout I've wanted, on principle as well as to show my gratitude, to credit honestly wherever appropriate, but I certainly wish to signal my thanks here as well. And if at any time a recipe has found its way onto these pages without having its source properly documented, I assure you and the putative unnamed originator that this is due to ignorance rather than villainy.

But if I question the tyranny of the recipe, that isn't to say I take a cavalier attitude. A recipe has to work. Even the great abstract painters have first to learn figure drawing. If many of my recipes seem to stretch out for a daunting number of pages, it is because brevity is no guarantee of simplicity. The easiest way to learn how to cook is by watching; and bearing that in mind I have tried more to talk you through a recipe than bark out instructions. As much as possible, I have wanted to make you feel that I'm there with you, in the kitchen, as you cook. The book that follows is the conversation we might be having.

Basics etc.

The Great Culinary Renaissance we hear so much about has done many things – given us extra virgin olive oil, better restaurants and gastroporn – but it hasn't taught us how to cook.

Of course standards have improved. Better ingredients are available to us now, and more people know about them. Food and cookery have become more than respectable: they are fashionable. But the renaissance of British cookery, as it was relentlessly tagged in the late 1980s, started in the restaurant and filtered its way into the home. This is the wrong way round. Cooking is best learned at your own stove: you learn by watching and by doing. Chefs themselves know this. The great chefs of France and Italy learn about food at home: what they do later, in the restaurants that make them famous, is use what they have learnt. They build on it, they start elaborating. They take home cooking to the restaurant, not the restaurant school of cookery to the home. Inverting the process is like learning a vocabulary without any grammar. The analogy is pertinent. In years as a restaurant critic, I couldn't help noticing that however fine the menu, some chefs, for all that they seem to have mastered the idiom, have no authentic language of their own. We are at risk, here, of becoming a land of culinary mimics. There are some things you just cannot learn from a professional chef. I am not talking of home economics – the rules that govern what food does when you apply heat or introduce air or whatever – but of home cooking, and of how experience builds organically. For there is more to cooking than being able to put on a good show. Of course there are advantages in an increased awareness of and enthusiasm for food, but the danger is that it excites an appetite for new recipes, new ingredients: follow a recipe once and then – on to the next. Cooking isn't like that. The point about real-life cooking is that your proficiency grows exponentially. You cook something once, then again, and again. Each time you add something different (leftovers from the fridge, whatever might be in the kitchen or in season) and what you end up with differs also.

You can learn how to cook fancy food from the colour supplements, but you need the basics. And anyway, it is better to be able to roast a chicken than to be a dab hand with focaccia. I would be exhausted if the cooking I did every day was recipe-index food. I don't want to cook like that all the time, and I certainly don't want to eat like that.

Nor do I want to go back to some notional golden age

of nursery food. I wasn't brought up on shepherd's pie and bread-and-butter pudding and I'm not going to start living on them now. It is interesting, though, that these homely foods have not been revived in our homes – they have been rediscovered by restaurants. And, even if I don't wish to eat this sort of thing all the time, isn't it more appropriate to learn how to cook it at home than to have to go to a restaurant to eat it?

By invoking the basics I certainly don't mean to evoke a grim, puritanical self-sufficiency, with austere recipes for home-made bread and stern admonishments against buying any form of food ready cooked. I have no wish to go on a crusade. I doubt I will ever become someone who habitually bakes her own bread – after all, shopping for good food is just as much of a pleasure as cooking it can be. But there is something between grinding your own flour and cooking only for special occasions. Cooking has become too much of a device by which to impress people rather than simply to feed them pleasurably.

In literature, teachers talk about key texts: they exist, too, in cooking. That's what I mean by basics.

Everyone's list of basics is, of course, different. Your idea of home cooking, your whole experience of eating, colours your sense of what foods should be included in the culinary canon. Cooking, indeed, is not so very different from literature: what you have read previously shapes how you read now. And so we eat; and so we cook.

If I don't include your nostalgic favourite in this chapter, you may find a recipe for it in *How to Eat*. And it is impossible to write a list without being painfully aware of what has been missed out: cooking is not an exclusive art, whatever its grander exponents might lead you to think. Being familiar with making certain dishes – so familiar that you don't need to look in a book to make them (and much of this chapter should eventually make itself redundant) – doesn't preclude you from cooking other things.

So what are basic dishes? Everyone has to know how to roast chicken, pork, beef, game, lamb: what to do with slabs of meat. This is not abstruse knowledge, but general information so basic that many books don't bother to mention it. I am often telephoned by friends at whose houses I have eaten something more elaborate than I would ever cook, to be asked how long their leg of lamb needs to be in the oven and at what temperature.

The key texts constitute the framework of your repertoire: stews, roasts, white sauce, mayonnaise, stocks, soups. You might also think of tackling pastry.

Because the English don't any longer have a firmly based culinary tradition – and, even at its solid best, English cookery never had anything like the range and variation of, say, regional French cooking – we tend to lack an enduring respect for particular dishes. It's not so much that we hunger to eat whatever is fashionable as that we drop anything that is no longer of the moment. The tendency is not exclusively English – if you were to go to a grand dinner party in France or Italy, you might be served whatever was considered the culinary *dernier cri* – but what makes our behaviour more emphatic, more ultimately sterile, is that we don't seem to cook any food other than style-conscious dinner-party food.

I think it is true, too, that we are quick to despise what once we looked at so breathlessly in colour supplements and delicatessens. Just because a food is no longer flavour of the month, it shouldn't follow that it is evermore to be spoken of as a shameful aberration. It is important always to judge honestly and independently. This can be harder than it sounds. Fashion has a curious but compelling urgency. Even those of us who feel we are free of fashion's diktats are, despite ourselves, influenced by them. As what is seemingly desirable changes, so our eye changes. It doesn't have to be wholesale conversion for this effect to take place: we just begin to look at things differently.

Of course, fashion may lead us to excesses. It is easy to ascribe the one-time popularity of nouvelle cuisine – which fashion decrees we must now treat as hootingly risible – to just such an excess. And to some extent that would be correct. But what some people forget is that the most ludicrous excesses of nouvelle cuisine were not follies committed by its most talented exponents but by the second and third rank. It is important to distinguish between what is fashionable and good and what is fashionable and bad.

With food it should be easier to maintain your integrity: you must, after all, always know whether you enjoy the taste of something or not. And in cooking as in eating, you just have to let your real likes and desires guide you.

My list of basics – and the recipes that constitute it – are dotted throughout this book. The list is eclectic. And in this chapter I have tried, in the main, to stay with the sort of food most of us anyway presume we can cook; it's only when we get started that we realise we need to look something up, check times, remind ourselves of the quantities. I want to satisfy those very basic demands without in any way wishing to make you feel as if there were some actual list of recipes which you needed to master before acquiring some notional and wholly goal-oriented culinary expertise. My aim is not to promote notions of uniformity or consistency – or even to imply that either might be desirable – but to suggest a way of cooking which isn't simply notching up recipes. In short, cooking in context.

First, you have to know how to do certain things, things that years ago it was taken for granted would be learned at home. These are ordinary kitchen skills, such as how to make pastry or a white sauce.

I learned some of these things with my mother in the kitchen when I was a child, but not all of them. So I understand the fearfulness that grips you just as you anticipate rolling out some shortcrust, say. We ate no puddings at home, my mother didn't bake and nor did my grandmothers. I didn't acquire early in life that lazy confidence, that instinct. When I cook a stew I have a sense, automatically, of whether I want to use red or white wine, of what will happen if I add anchovies or bacon. But when I bake I feel I lack that instinct, though I hope I am beginning to acquire it.

And of course I have faltered, made mistakes, cooked disasters. I know what it's like to panic in the kitchen, to feel flustered by a recipe which lists too many ingredients or takes for granted too much expertise or dexterity.

I don't think the answer, though, is to avoid anything that seems, on first view, complicated or involves elaborate procedures. That just makes you feel more fearful. But what is extraordinarily liberating is trying something – say, pastry – and finding out that, left quietly to your own devices, you can actually do it. What once seemed an arcane skill becomes second nature. It does happen.

And how it happens is by repetition. If you haven't made pastry before, follow the recipe for shortcrust on page 30. Make a flan. Don't leave it too long to make another one. Or a pie or a savoury tart. The point is to get used gradually to cooking something in the ordinary run of things. I concede that it might mean having to make more of a conscious effort in the beginning, but the time and concentration needed will recede naturally, and the effort will soon cease altogether to be conscious. It will just become part of what you do.

Basic roast chicken

You could probably get through life without knowing how to roast a chicken, but the question is, would you want to?

When I was a child we had roast chicken at Saturday lunch, and probably one evening a week, too. Even when there were only a few of us, my mother never roasted just one chicken; she cooked two, one to keep in the fridge, cold and whole, for picking at during the week. It's partly for that reason that a roast chicken, to me, smells of home, of family, of food that carries some important, extra-culinary weight.

My basic roast chicken is the same as my mother's: I stick half a lemon up its bottom, smear some oil or butter on its breast, sprinkle it with a little salt, and put it in a gas mark 6/200°C oven for about 20 minutes per 500g plus 30 minutes.

My mother could make the stringiest, toughest flesh – a bird that had been intensively farmed and frozen since the last Ice Age – taste as if it were a lovingly reared poulet de Bresse. She, you see, was a product of her age, which believed that cooking lay in what you did to inferior products (and I expect she did no more in this case than use much more butter than anyone would now); I, however, am a product of mine, which believes that you always use the best, the freshest produce of the highest quality you can afford – and then do as little as possible to it. So I buy organic free-range chickens and anoint them with the tiniest amount of extra virgin olive oil or butter – as if I were

You could probably get through life without knowing how to roast a chicken, but the question is, would you want to?

putting on very expensive handcream – before putting them in the oven. I retain the lemon out of habit – and to make my kitchen smell like my mother's, with its aromatic, oily-sharp fug.

I can't honestly say that my roast chicken tastes better than hers, but I don't like eating intensively farmed, battery-reared meat. However, if you know you've got an inferior bird in front of you, cook it for the first hour breast side down. This means you don't, at the end, have quite that glorious effect of the swelling, burnished breast – the chicken will have more of a flapper's bosom, flat but fleshy – but the white meat will be more tender because all the fats and juices will have oozed their way into it.

If you want to make a good gravy – and I use the term to indicate a meat-thick golden juice or, risking pretentiousness here, *jus* – then put 1 tablespoon of olive oil in the roasting dish when you anoint the bird before putting it in the oven, and about half an hour before the end add another tablespoon of oil and a spritz from the lemon half that isn't stuffed up the chicken. By all means use butter if you prefer, but make sure there's some oil in the pan, too, to stop the butter from burning.

When you remove the chicken, let it stand for 5 or 10 minutes before carving it, and make gravy by putting the roasting dish on the hob (remove, if you want, any excess fat with a spoon, though I tend to leave it as it is). Add a little white wine and boiling water or chicken stock, letting it all bubble away till it's syrupy and chickeny. If you don't have to hand any home-made stock a stock cube, or portion thereof, would be fine. In fact, Italians sometimes put a stock cube inside the chicken along with or instead of the lemon half before roasting it.

My basic chicken recipe also includes garlic and shallots; this is the easy way to have dinner on the table without doing much. About 50 minutes before the end of the cooking time, pour 2 tablespoons olive oil either into the same pan or another one and add the unpeeled cloves of 2 heads of garlic and about 20 unpeeled shallots. They don't roast, really, but steam inside their skins, which on the garlic are like boiled-sweet wrappers, on the shallots like twists of brown paper. Eat them by pressing on them with a fork, and letting the soft, mild – that's to say intensely flavoured and yet wholly without pungency – creamy interior squeeze out on to your plate. Put some plates on the table for the discarded skins, and if not finger bowls then napkins or a roll of paper towel. My children adore garlic and shallots cooked like this, and sometimes, when I don't want to cook a whole chicken for them, I roast a poussin instead and put the shallots and garlic and poussin in all at the same time. And if you want to make this basic recipe feel a little less basic, then you can sprinkle some toasted pine nuts and flat-leaf parsley, chopped at the last minute, over the food before serving.

If you've managed to fit the garlic and shallots in the tray with the chicken, you can roast a tray of potatoes in the same oven at the same time. Dice the potatoes, also unpeeled, into approximately 1cm cubes, or just cut new potatoes in half lengthways, and anoint them with oil (or melted lard, which fries them fabulously crisp). Sprinkle them with a little dried thyme (or freshly chopped rosemary) before cooking them for 1 hour to 1 hour 10 minutes.

All of which leads us to the next basic recipe:

Stock

Do not throw away the chicken carcass after eating the chicken. Go so far, I'd say, as to scavenge from everyone's plate, picking up the bones they've left. I'm afraid I even do this in other people's houses. You don't need to make stock now – and indeed you couldn't make anything very useful from the amount of bones from one bird – but freeze them. Indeed freeze whatever bones you can, whenever you can, in order to make stock at some later date (see page 47 for further, passionate, adumbration of this thesis).

An actual recipe for stock would be hard to give with a straight face; boiling remains up to make stock is as far from being a precise art as you can get. There are recipes in *How to Eat* for broth and consommé if you want something highfalutin', but if you're looking for what I call chicken stock (but which classically trained French chefs, who would use fresh meat and raw bones, boiled up specifically to make stock, would most definitely not), then follow my general instructions. At home, I would use the carcasses of 3 medium, cooked chickens.

Break the bones up roughly and put them in a big pan. Add a stick of celery broken in two or a few lovage leaves, 1 or 2 carrots, depending on size, peeled and halved, 1 onion stuck with a clove, 5 peppercorns, a bouquet garni, some parsley stalks and the white of a leek. Often I have more or less everything to hand without trying, except for that leek; in which case I just leave it out. (At the time of writing, it is still permitted to buy veal shin, and I sometimes add a couple of discs if I want a deeper-toned broth of almost unctuous mellowness.) Cover with cold water, add 1 teaspoon of salt and bring to the boil, skimming off the froth and scum that rises to the surface. Lower the heat and let the stock bubble very, very gently, uncovered, for about 3 hours. Allow to cool a little, then strain into a wide, large bowl or another pan. When cold, put in the fridge without decanting yet. I like to let it chill in the fridge so that I can remove any fat that rises to the surface, and the wider that surface is, the easier.

When I've removed the fat, I taste the stock and consider whether I'd prefer it stronger flavoured. If so, I put it back in a pan on the hob and boil it down till I've got a smaller amount of rich, intensely flavoured stock.

I then store it in differing quantities in the freezer. On the whole, the amount of stock I find most useful is in packages of 150ml and 300ml. For the smaller amount, I just ladle ten tablespoons into a freezer bag or small tub with a lid; for the larger, I line a measuring jug with a freezer bag and pour it in till I've got, give or take, 300ml (it's difficult, because of the baggy lining, to judge with super-calibrated accuracy). I then twist on the tie-up and put the whole thing, jug and all, into the freezer. This is why I own so many plastic measuring jugs. I am constantly forgetting about them once they're buried in the freezer. But, in principle, what you should do is leave the stock till solid, then whisk away the jug, leaving the jug-shaped cylinder of frozen liquid, which you slot back into the deep-freeze. You may need to run hot water over the jug for a minute in order to let the stock in its bag just slip out. This is a useful way to freeze any liquid. Although it's a bore, it pays to measure accurately and to label clearly at the time of freezing. Later you can take out exactly the quantity you need.

Poussins make wonderful, strong, easily jellied stock; it must be the amount of zip and gelatin in their poor young bones. So if ever you need to make a stock from scratch, with fresh meat, not cooked bones (in other words the way you're supposed to), and you can't find a boiling fowl, then buy some poussins, about 4, cut each in half, use vegetables as above, cover with cold water and proceed as normal.

And I do not disapprove of stock cubes, if they're good.

One of the most useful things an Italian friend once showed me was how important even half a stick of celery is in providing base-note flavour, not just to stocks, but to tomato and meat sauces, to pies, in fact to almost anything savoury. The taste is not boorishly celery-like; it just provides an essential floor of flavour.

In Italy, when you buy vegetables from the greengrocer you can ask for a bunch of *odori*, which is a bunch of those herbs which breathe their essential scent into sauces and is given, gratis. Included in it will be one stick of celery. And I wish we could buy, let alone get for free, celery by the single stick in Britain. You need so little of it when cooking, and most of what's on sale anyway – white, limp and waterlogged – scarcely repays the eating. If I can get huge, leafy, green Spanish or Italian celery, I mind less about having to buy a whole bunch; apart from anything else it looks beautiful in a vase in the kitchen. But those leaf-stripped, bendy-stalked clumps of waxy-white celery that are normally on sale, especially in the supermarkets, are the saddest of dismal forced-hand purchases.

You should grow your own herbs if you can and want to, but don't spread yourself, or your plants, too thinly. It is counter-productive if you have so little of each herb that you never pick much of it for fear of totally denuding your stock. In my own garden, I stick to rosemary, flat-leaf parsley, rocket and sorrel. I like to grow lots of parsley – at least two rows, the length of the whole bed – and even more rocket. Some years I've planted garlic so that I can use the gloriously infused leaves, as they grow, cut up freshly in a salad. In pots I keep bay, marjoram and mint. This year I'm going to try some angelica – to flavour custards – and Thai basil, so that I don't have to go to the Thai shop to buy huge bunches of the stuff, wonderfully aromatic though it is, only to see it go off before I've had a chance to use it all. I have never had any success with coriander (from seed). I can manage basil easily, but then I suddenly feel overrun. And I have to say, I find watering pots excruciatingly effortful.

As with so much to do with food, a lot of a little rather than a little of a lot is the best, most comforting and most useful rule. You can always buy herbs growing in pots, in season, at good supermarkets and garden centres, and herbs cut in big bunches in specialist shops and good greengrocers.

Mayonnaise

Stock is what you may make out of the bones of your roasted chicken, but mayonnaise, real mayonnaise, is what you might make to eat with the cold, leftover meat. There is one drawback: when you actually make mayonnaise you realise, beyond the point of insistent denial, how much oil goes into it. But since even the best bottled mayonnaise bears little or no relation to real mayonnaise, you may as well know how to make it. And it really isn't difficult.

When I was in my teens, I loved Henry James. I read him with uncorrupted pleasure. Then, when I was eighteen or so, and had just started *The Golden Bowl*, someone – older, cleverer, whose opinions were offered gravely – asked me whether I didn't find James very difficult, as she always did. Until then, I had no idea that I might, and I didn't. From that moment, I couldn't read him but self-consciously; from then on, I did find him difficult. I do not wish to insult by the comparison, but I had a similar, Jamesian mayonnaise experience. My mother used to make mayonnaise weekly, twice weekly; we children would help. I had no idea it was meant to be difficult, or that it was thought to be such a nerve-racking ordeal. Then someone asked how I managed to be so breezy about it, how I stopped it from curdling. From then on, I scarcely made a mayonnaise which didn't split. It's not surprising: when confidence is undermined or ruptured, it can be difficult to do the simplest things, or to take any enjoyment even in trying.

I don't deny that mayonnaises can split, but please don't jinx yourself. Anyway, it's not a catastrophe if it does. A small drop of boiling water can fix things, and if it doesn't, you can start again with an egg yolk in a bowl. Beat it and slowly beat in the curdled mess of mayo you were previously working on. Later add more oil and a little lemon juice. You should, this way, end up with the smoothly amalgamated yellow ointment you were after in the first place. I hate to say it, but you may have to do this twice. You may end up with rather more mayonnaise than you need, but getting it right in the end restores your confidence, and this is the important thing.

I make mayonnaise the way my mother did: I warm the eggs in the bowl (as explained more fully later) then beat and add oil just from the bottle, not measuring, until the texture feels right, feels like mayonnaise. I squeeze in lemon juice, also freehand, until the look and taste feel right. If you make a habit of making mayonnaise, you will inevitably come to judge it instinctively too. I don't like too much olive oil in it: if it's too strong it rasps the back of the throat, becomes too invasive. I use a little over two-thirds groundnut oil and a little under one-third olive oil, preferably that lovely mild stuff from Liguria. If you prefer, do use half and half and a mild French olive oil, which is probably more correct, anyway, than the Italian variety.

By habit, and maternal instruction, I always used to use an ordinary whisk. This takes a long time (and I can see why my mother used us, her children, as *commis* chefs). Now I use my KitchenAid (similar to a Kenwood Chef, but American) with the wire whip in place. You can equally well use one of those electric hand-held whisks, which are cheap and useful. Please, whatever you do, don't use a food processor: if you do, your finished product tastes just like the gluey bought stuff. And then, hell, you might as well just go out and buy it.

2 egg yolks (but wait to separate the eggs, and see below)
225ml groundnut or sunflower oil
75ml extra virgin olive oil
juice of ½ lemon

Put the eggs, in their shells, in a large bowl. Fill it with warm water from the tap and leave for 10 minutes. (This brings eggs and bowl comfortably to room temperature, which will help stop the eggs from curdling, but is optional, as long as you remember to take the eggs out of the fridge well before you need them.) Then remove the eggs, get rid of the water and dry the bowl thoroughly. Wet and then wring out a tea towel and set the bowl on it; this stops it slipping and jumping about on the worksurface.

Separate the eggs. Put aside the whites and freeze them for another use, and let the yolks plop into the dried bowl. Start whisking the yolks with a pinch of salt. After a few minutes very, very gradually and drop by mean drop, add the groundnut oil. You must not rush this. It's easier to let the oil seep in gradually if you pour from a height, holding the measuring jug (or bottle with a spout attached, if you're not actually using measured quantities) well above the bowl. Keep going until you see a thick mayonnaise form, about 2–3 tablespoons' worth, then you can relax and let the oil drip in small glugs. When both oils have been incorporated (first the groundnut, then the olive oil) and you have a thick, smooth, firm mayonnaise, add a few squeezes of lemon juice, whisking all the time. Taste to see if you need to add more. Add salt and pepper as you like; my mother used white pepper, so she didn't end up with black specks.

Vinaigrette

One of the hangovers of the hostess-trolley age is the idea that the clever cook has a secret vinaigrette recipe which can transform the dullest lettuce into a Sensational Salad. I'm not sure I even have a regular vinaigrette recipe, let alone one with a winning, magic ingredient. But we all panic in the kitchen from time to time, so here is a useful, broad-brush reminder of how to compose a salad.

Plain salad dressing

I sometimes think the best way of dressing salad is to use just oil and lemon juice. The trick is to use the best possible olive oil – and as little of it as possible – and toss it far longer than you'd believe possible. Use your hands for this. Start off with 1 tablespoon of oil for a whole bowl of lettuce and keep tossing, adding more oil only when you are convinced the leaves need it. When all the leaves are barely covered with the thinnest film of oil, sprinkle over a scant ½ teaspoon sea salt. Toss again. Then squeeze over some lemon juice. Give a final fillip, then taste and adjust as necessary. Instead of lemon juice you can substitute wine vinegar (and I use red wine vinegar rather than white generally), but be sparing. Just as the perfect martini, it was always said, was made merely by tilting the vermouth bottle in the direction of the gin, so when making the perfect dressing you should merely point the cork of the vinegar bottle towards the oil.

As important is the composition of the salad itself. Keep it simple: there's a green salad, which is green; or there's a red salad, of tomatoes (and maybe onions). First-course salads may be granted a little extra leeway – the addition of something warm and sautéed – but I would never let a tomato find its way into anything leafy. For more detailed explanations (genetic as much as aesthetic) of this prejudice, please see page 95. When you're using those already-mixed packets of designer leaves, you should add one crunchy lettuce – cos or Webb – which you buy, radically and separately, as a lettuce and then tear up yourself at the last minute. Herbs – parsley, chives, chervil, lovage – are a good idea in a green salad (and you can add them either to the salad or the dressing), but, except on certain, rare, occasions, I think garlic is better left out.

Bread

BREAD IS BASIC in the staff-of-life sense, but making it is hardly a fundamental activity for most of us. I don't get the urge that often, but every time I have, and have consulted a suitable book, I have been directed to make wholemeal bread. You may as well bake hessian. Why should it be thought that only those who want wholemeal bread are the sort to bake their own? Good wholemeal bread is very hard to make, and I suspect needs heavy machinery or enormous practice and muscularity.

Anyway, I give you this recipe for old-fashioned white bread, really good white bread, the sort you eat with unsalted butter and jam – one loaf in a sitting, no trouble. The recipe comes from Foster's Bakery in Barnsley, South

Yorkshire, and found its way to me at a breadmaking workshop given at the Flour Advisory Board in London by John Foster. He was an exceptional teacher, and completely turned me, a lifelong sceptic of the breadmaking tendency, into a would-be baker.

Basic white loaf

For a good white loaf such as even I can make convincingly – a small one, so double the quantities if you want a big loaf or a couple – you need:

300g strong flour
10g fresh yeast
10g salt (1 heaped teaspoon)
5g sugar (½ 1 teaspoon)
170ml tepid water
10g fat

Buy the best flour you can (and there are plenty of good mills in this country, most of which sell their flours through health stores) and use real yeast, not dried. Before you get put off, you should know two things. The first is that you can buy real yeast at any baker's, including the in-store bakeries of supermarkets; the second is that you use the real yeast here as you would easy-blend instant yeast – there's no frothing or blending or anything, you just add it to the mound of flour.

So: tip the flour onto a worktop and add the yeast, salt and sugar. Pour over the water and bring together, working with one hand, clawing at the floury mess rather as if your hand were a spider and your fingers the spider's legs. The spider analogy is apposite: you do have to be a bit 'If at first you don't suceed, try,

try again' about bread-making. As the dough starts to come together, add the fat – which can be lard (my favourite here), vegetable shortening or oil – and keep squishing with your hands. When the dough has come together, begin kneading. Do this by stretching the dough away from you and working it into the worktop. Rub a little flour into your hands to remove any bits of dough that stick.

Keep kneading, pressing the heel of your hand into the dough, pushing the dough away, bringing it back and down against the work surface, for at least 10 minutes. John Foster warns that after 5 minutes you'll want to give up, and he's right. He suggests singing a song to keep yourself going; I prefer listening to the radio or talking to someone, but maybe that's just the difference between northerner and southerner.

When the dough's properly mixed – after about 10 minutes – you can tell the difference; it suddenly feels smoother and less sticky. Bring it to a ball, flour the worktop and the piece of dough lightly, and cover with a plastic bag or sheet of clingfilm and a tea-towel and leave for 30 minutes.

Then knead again for 3 minutes. Flour the worktop and dough ball again, cover as before, and leave for another 30 minutes.

Flatten the dough to expel the gas bubbles. Fold it in half, then in half again, and again, and keep folding the dough over itself until it feels as if you can fold no longer, as if the dough itself resists it (rather than you can't bear it) and then shape it into a ball again. Flour the worktop and so forth, cover the dough and leave, this time for 10 minutes.

Then shape the dough as you want: either round or oval and smooth, or you can slash the top with a knife, or put in a greased

450g loaf tin. Now, place on the baking tray (or in its tin) and put it in a warm place, under a plastic bag, for an hour, before baking for 35 minutes in a preheated gas mark 8/220°C oven. The trick is to lift the bread up and knock the base; if it sounds hollow, it's cooked. Try to let the bread cool before eating it.

You can do the final proving in the fridge overnight (technically this is known as retarding). This doesn't cut out any work, but I find it makes things easier because I can do all the kneading when the children are in bed and before I go to bed (incidentally, it is, if not exactly calming, certainly very stress-relieving) and then bake the bread when I get up.

You do, however, need to increase the amount of yeast for this. Exactly how much you need to increase it by will depend on your fridge and the nature of your yeast. This may not be helpful, but it's true. Try doubling the yeast to 20g, then if the bread bolts when it's in the oven, you'll know to use 15g next time. When you get up in the morning preheat the oven, taking the bread out of the fridge on its baking tray as you do so. Leave it for 10 minutes or so, and then bake as above, maybe giving it an extra couple of minutes.

Pastry

On the subject of pastry, I am positively evangelical. Until fairly recently I practised heavy avoidance techniques, hastily, anxiously turning away from any recipe which included pastry, as if the cookbook's pages themselves were burning: I was hot with fear; could feel the flush rise in my panicky cheeks. I take strength from that, and so should you. Because if I can do the culinary equivalent, for me, of Learning to Love the Bomb, so can you.

It came upon me gradually. I made some plain shortcrust pastry, alone and in silence, apart from the comforting wall of voices emanating from Radio 4: it worked; I made some more. Then I tried some pâte sucrée: it worked; I made some more; it didn't. But the next time, it did; or rather, I dealt better with its difficulties. But shortcrust, or even rich shortcrust, is really easy, and that's all you need to know.

Shortcrust

At its simplest, pastry is just a quantity of flour mixed with half its weight in fat and bound with water.

So, to make enough plain shortcrust to line and cover a 23cm pie dish (in other words for a double-crust pie), you would mix 240g flour with 120g cold, diced fat (half lard or vegetable shortening and half butter for preference), rubbing the fat in with your fingertips until you have a bowl of floury breadcrumb or oatmeal-sized flakes. Then you add iced water until the flour and fat turn into a ball of dough; a few tablespoons should do it. But as simple as that is, I can make it simpler; or rather, I can make it easier, as easy as it can be.

The first way to do this is not to use our ordinary plain flour but Italian 00 flour. This is the flour Italians at home, rather than in factories, use for pasta and it's certainly true that it seems to give pastry an almost pasta-like elasticity.

The second part of my facilitation programme is as follows.

Measure the flour into a bowl and add the cold fat, cut into 1cm dice. You then put this, as is, in the freezer for 10 minutes. Then you put it in the food processor with the double blade attached or into a food mixer with the paddle attached, and switch on (at slow to medium speed if you're using the mixer) until the mixture resembles oatmeal. Then you add, tablespoon by cautious tablespoon, the iced water, to which you've added a squeeze of lemon and a pinch of salt. I find you need a little more liquid when making pastry by this method than you do when the flour and fat haven't had that chilling burst in the deep-freeze.

When the dough looks as if it's about to come together, but just before it actually does, you turn off all machinery, remove the dough, divide into two and form each half into a ball, flatten the balls into fat discs, and cover these discs with clingfilm or put them each inside a freezer bag, and shove them in the fridge for 20 minutes. This makes pastry anyone could roll out, even if you add too much liquid by mistake.

Now, this method relies on a machine to make the pastry. To tell the truth, I culled and simplified the technique from a fascinating book, *Cookwise*, by an American food scientist called Shirley O. Corriher, and she does all sorts of strenuous things, including making the pastry by tipping out the freezer-chilled flour and fat onto a cold surface and battering it with a rolling pin until it looks like 'paint-flakes that have fallen off a wall'. She does, however, sanction the use of a mixer bowl (well-chilled) and paddle (set on slowest speed) and I have found, as described above, that it works well in the processor too. I know that I am not up to her hand-rolling method, or not yet at any rate.

Foods in Season

DON'T BELIEVE EVERYTHING you're told about the greater good of eating foods only when they are in season. The purists may be right, but being right isn't everything. If you live in the Tuscan hills, you may find different lovely things to eat every month of the year, but for us it would mean having to subsist half the time on a diet of tubers and cabbage, so why shouldn't we be grateful that we live in the age of jet transport and extensive culinary imports? More smug guff is spoken on this subject than almost anything else.

There is no doubt that there are concomitant drawbacks: the food is out of kilter with the climate in which it is eaten; it's picked underripe and transported in the wrong conditions; the intense pleasure of eating something when it comes into its own season is lost; the relative merits, the particular properties of individual fruits and vegetables are submerged in the greedy zeal of the tantrumming adult who must Have It Now. There's no point in eating flown-in asparagus which tastes of nothing (though not all of it does), or peaches in December, ripe-looking but jade-fleshed. But my life is improved considerably by the fact that I can go to my greengrocer's and routinely buy stuff I would otherwise have to go to Italy to find.

I love fresh peas, but they aren't the high point of our culinary year for me. Once they get to the shops, all that pearly sugariness has pretty well turned to starch anyway. As far as I'm concerned, the foods whose short season it would be criminal to ignore are:

rhubarb, the forced, best and pinkest: January–February
Seville oranges: January–February
purple-sprouting broccoli: February–March
home-grown asparagus: May–June
elderflowers: June
grouse: 12 August–10 December
damsons: August–September
quinces: November–December
white truffles: November–January

Rhubarb

I know many people are put off rhubarb because of vile experiences in childhood. I have faith, however, or rather passionate hope, that I can overcome this prejudice. And since my own childhood contained little traditional nursery food, it takes on, for me, something of the exotic. My adult love affair with rhubarb is heady illustration of this.

Seville oranges

You can now buy Seville oranges in supermarkets, but they are regarded almost exclusively as for making marmalade. This is such a waste. Seville oranges have the fragrance and taste of oranges but the sourness of lemons. Try them, then, wherever you'd use lemons – to squirt over fish, to squeeze into salad dressings, to use in a buttery hollandaise-like sauce or in mayonnaise to eat with cold duck. A squeeze of Seville orange is pretty divine in black tea, too. And although you can only buy them in January or early February, they freeze well.

Traditionally, oranges go with duck: real canard à l'orange should be made with bitter and not sweet oranges; you shouldn't end up with jam. Put half a Seville orange up the bottom of a mallard and squeeze the other half, mixed with 1 teaspoon honey or sesame oil, as you wish, over the breast before you cook it. Roast in a hot gas mark 7/210°C oven for 40 minutes. You won't even need to deglaze the pan to make a sauce to go with the mallard: the juices there will be good enough just as they are, though if you wish you can add more Seville orange juice, sweetened with honey to taste or left sharp. If you want something more sauce-like, thicken with 1 teaspoon cornflour, made first into a paste with some of the juice.

Scallops have been cooked with bitter oranges since the eighteenth century. You can do a modern turn on the same theme simply by sautéing each glorious white disc (remove the coral for the time being) in bacon fat, butter or olive oil, 1 minute or so each side, before removing and deglazing the pan with a good squirt of Seville orange juice. Make sure you've also got enough juices in the pan to make a dressing for the watercress with which you're going to line the plate.

If they make up supper in its entirety, I'd get about 5 scallops per head. If you want to eat the corals with the scallops, then fry them for about thirty seconds after you've removed the fleshy rounds, or freeze them to fry up later with a lot of minced garlic to eat, alone and greedily, spread on toast.

Purple-sprouting broccoli

Purple-sprouting broccoli is avoided by those who think that good food has to be fancy. Clearly they don't deserve it.

Steam or lightly boil it and eat as you would asparagus, dipped into hollandaise, into plain melted butter (with or without breadcrumbs fried with it) or into a sharp, semi-emulsified sauce made by warming through some finely chopped anchovy fillets in wonderful olive oil. There can't be a wrong way to eat broccoli; just with soy sauce is fine enough.

I like a plate of sprouting broccoli mixed with asparagus (imported – it has to be). They make a good couple.

Asparagus

English asparagus is expensive in restaurants and easy to cook well at home. Don't worry about special asparagus pans, just cook the asparagus in abundant boiling salted water in a pan or couple of pans which are wide and big enough for the whole spears, stem, tip and all, to be submerged. Cook for 3–5 minutes (test and taste regularly – it's better to waste some spears than for them to be either woody or soggy) and drain thoroughly, first in the colander and then lying flat on the draining board, but do it gently, too: you want the spears to stay beautiful and remain intact.

The usual accompaniment, and always a successful one, is hollandaise, but often I like to do something more homey and give each person a boiled egg in an eggcup for them to dip their asparagus into, like bread-and-butter soldiers. The eggs have to be perfectly soft-boiled; there is no room whatsoever for error. I don't wish to frighten you, but it's the truth. Provide 2 per person and smash or cut the tops off each as soon as they're cooked.

If you feel safer with a non-traditional method, then roll the asparagus in a little olive oil, then roast it, laid out on a tray, in a seriously preheated gas mark 8/220°C oven for 15–20 minutes. When cooked, the spears should be wilted and turning sweet and brown at the tips. Sprinkle over some coarse salt, arrange on a big plate and line another big plate with thin slices of prosciutto (San Daniele or Parma). Let people pick up the hot, soft, blistered spears using the ham to wrap around the asparagus like the finest rosy silk-damask napkins.

Elderflowers

You don't need to have a vast estate with elderflowers springing lacily to flower from that avenue of trees lining the drive; just pick them roadside whenever you see them.

I don't normally go in for individual puddings, each precious darling to be ceremoniously unmoulded from its ramekin. But I make an exception here, would have to. This is, in effect, *panna cotta*, and as with the Italian pudding, this very English-tasting cream needs to be set with as little gelatine as possible. I've tried with big moulds and just can't set it enough without turning it half-way into rubber. These are perfection as they are, and anyway, I use a mixture of teacups, sticky-toffee-pudding moulds and ramekins, feeling that the pleasurable lack of uniformity makes up for any potential dinkiness. Line the moulds, cups and so on with clingfilm, pushing it well against the corners and over the rim so you've got a tuggable edge; it may make for the odd wrinkle or crease on the surface of the set cream, but that doesn't matter; what does is that you will be able to unmould them easily.

900ml double cream
18 heads of elderflower
6 tablespoons caster sugar
9.5g leaf gelatine

Heat cream over low heat in saucepan with the elderflowers. When it comes bubbling to a simmering near-boil, turn it off, remove from the heat and cover. Leave for up to a couple of hours, but not less than ½ hour, to infuse. Then stir in the sugar and bring back to boiling point. Taste to see if more sugar is needed and then sieve into a jug. While the last of the headily aromatic cream is dripping off the elderflowers, soak the leaves of gelatine in cold water. In 5 minutes or so, when the gelatine is softened, squeeze the leaves out and then beat into the warm cream in the jug. Make sure they are dissolved and dispersed and pour into the clingfilm-lined moulds. Cool and then put in the fridge overnight.

With these serve a contrastingly lumpy bowl of gooseberries: the Victorians knew well, and invoked often, the muscatty aptness of the combination of elderflower and gooseberry; about many things they were wrong; about this they were right. Put 750g gooseberries in a pan with 350ml water and 6 tablespoons of sugar. Bring it all to the boil and simmer for a couple of minutes. Drain, reserving syrup, then put the fruit in a bowl and return the lightly syrupy juices to the pan. Bring it to the boil again and let boil for 5 minutes. Pour it into a bowl or jug to cool, while the fruit cools separately in its bowl, then when you're about it eat, put the gooseberries in a shallow dish and cover with the syrup.

Grouse

Grouse should either be roasted plain, first smeared thickly with butter, in a gas mark 6/200°C oven for 30–45 minutes (the size of the birds varies, but you want the flesh to be rubied and juicy, but not underdone to the point of tough quiveriness) and eaten with bread sauce, or stuffed with thyme and mascarpone (yes, really).

Damsons

Damsons are a glorious fruit. They can't be eaten raw and are a chore to prepare and cook, but it's only once a year . . .

I sometimes make damson ice-cream, but damson fool is the recipe for which I wait most greedily. This fool is not difficult to make, but it is stunning, utterly distinctive: you can taste in it both the almost metallic depth of the sour fruit and billowy sweetness of the bulky cream. And it's wonderful after grouse.

500g damsons
2 teaspoons each dark muscovado, light muscovado and caster sugar
¼ teaspoon mixed ground spice
300ml double cream, whipped with 2 tablespoons icing sugar

Put the whole damsons (try to stone them now and you'll go really mad) in a pan with 125ml water and the sugars, bring to the boil and cook till soft. Push through a sieve or food mill to get rid of the stones and add the spice and more sugar to taste if you think it's needed.

When cool, stir into the sugar-whipped cream and pour either into individual pots or into a bowl. This will fill 6 glasses of the sort you'd eat pudding from, but if you're putting the fool in a bowl then count on feeding only 4.

Quinces

Quince, the apple which Paris presented to Helen and maybe even the one which grew in the garden of Eden (although there is, it's argued, a more convincing academic case to be made for the pomegranate here) is a ravishing mixture of *One Thousand and One Nights* exotic and Victorian kitchen homeliness. It looks like a mixture between apple and pear, but tastes like neither. And actually the taste is not the point: what this fruit is all about is heady, perfect fragrance. I have something of an obsession for quinces, although they are in the shops only for a scant eight weeks, aren't at all easy to deal with and can't be eaten raw. In the old days, quinces were kept in airing cupboards to perfume the linen, pervading the house with their honeyed but sharp aroma, so you needn't feel bad if you buy a bowlful and then just watch them rot in a kitchen or wherever.

You should add a quince, peeled, cored and sliced or chunked to apple pie or crumble. Poach them in muscat or make mostarda. Although I am not someone who goes in for preserve-making, I do make mostarda.

There's mostarda di Cremona, which has become modishly familiar over here, those stained-glass-window-coloured gleaming pots of fruits glossily preserved in mustard oil: no one, even in Italy apparently, makes their own. But mostarda di Venezia is different. You can't buy it and it's easy to make. It's just quinces boiled up with white wine, with the addition of sugar, candied peel and mustard powder. It's wonderful with any cold meat (which makes it very useful for Christmas and, since you have to leave it a month or so before eating, rather well timed for it, too). I also risk a culinary culture-clash by eating it alongside couscous and curries. Or you can eat it with a dollop of mascarpone, sweetened and flavoured with rum, as pudding.

This recipe is adapted from the one in Anna Del Conte's *The Classic Food of Northern Italy* which, as these things do, has a mixed parentage of its own. I have changed it a little. I simplify the procedure (see below) and also make it hotter and with almost double the amount of candied peel. Now, I loathe and detest commercial candied peel, but it's different here, not least because you must not use the ready-diced, bitter and oversweet at the same time, vile stuff in tubs. Seach out the good candied peel, whole, in large jars.

The second time I made mostarda di Venezia I didn't peel and core the quinces. It's such hard work. Instead I just roughly chopped the fruit and then, when cooked, pushed the lot through a fine food mill. Laziness prompted this modification, but since the peel and core help the set and intensify the flavour, you should have no qualms. If you don't own a mouli-légumes I suppose you could just push the fruit through a sieve, but that's strenuous too. So if you don't own this cheap and useful piece of equipment, it would be easier to peel, quarter and core to start with.

1.8kg quinces
1 bottle (750ml) white wine
grated rind and juice of 1 unwaxed lemon
sugar (1–1.2kg, see below)
8 tablespoons English mustard powder
250g candied peel (see above), cut into small cubes

Roughly chop the quinces, put them in a pan and cover them with the wine. Add the lemon rind and juice and cook until soft, about 40 minutes. Purée the mixture by pushing it through a food mill, weigh and add the same weight in sugar. Return to the pan. Dissolve the mustard powder in a little hot water and add to the purée with 1 teaspoon salt and the candied peel. Cook gently until the liquid is reduced and the mostarda becomes dense and, normally, deeper-coloured, about 20–30 minutes.

Sterilise some jars (I find the dishwasher's performance adequate) and fill with the mostarda. When it is cool, cover, seal and store away. Keep for about a month before you use it.

What you should also know about quinces is that for all their hardness, they bruise very easily. Whenever I have got a batch of quinces, at least a third of them have been riddled within with speckles, or worse, of what looks like rust. I just ignore it, unless of course it's obviously rotten. Anyway, quinces darken as they cook, going from glassy-yellow to coral to deepest, burnt terracotta; the odd bit of bruising really won't show.

White truffles

No greedy person's mention of foods in season could ignore the white truffle. I don't really understand the fuss about black truffles, but a white truffle – called by Rossini the Mozart of funghi – is something else. You don't do anything to it. You just shave it. And if you're buying a truffle you may as well go the whole hog and buy the thing with which to shave it over a plate of buttery egg pasta or into an equally rich risotto made with good broth. It is instant culinary nirvana. And although expensive, so much less so, unbelievably less so, than eating it in a restaurant.

Freezer

I LIVED FOR YEARS without a freezer without ever minding very much. Certainly this allowed me the luxury of dreaming of all the goods things I would cook and put by should I ever have one: I imagined with pleasure the efficient domestic angel I would then become. Now that I do have a freezer, and a big American one to boot, it is indeed full. And, yet, I feel faintly resentful of its fullness.

The difficulty I find with stuffing a freezer full of food to eat at some future date is that when that future date comes I probably won't want to eat it. This is not because the food will spoil or disappoint, but because every time I open my freezer I see the same efficiently-stowed-away packets of coq au vin or beef stew or whatever it may be, and I get bored with them. I begin to feel as if I've eaten them as many times as I've opened the freezer door.

The freezer can easily become a culinary graveyard, a place where good food goes to die.

If you're someone who is meticulous about cooking, freezing, filing and then thawing in an orderly fashion, you need no advice from me as to how best to use your freezer. But you must be honest with yourself. There is no point in stowing away stews and soups if you are going to let them linger so long in its depths that finally all you can do is chuck them out. You'll probably find you stand more chance of eating the food you cook in advance if – when you put it in the freezer – you do so with some particular occasion in mind rather than just stashing it away for some unspecified future time. Obviously, if you know people are coming for dinner on Friday but the only time you can get any cooking done is on the weekend before, then the freezer will be useful (see Cooking in Advance). But unless you have an astonishingly capacious freezer and a mania for planning in advance, I wouldn't advise stocking up for more than one or two such occasions at any one time. However, there are occasions in which even I am ruthlessly efficient about freezing and then using food: cooking for children is unimaginably easier if you create a form of culinary database in the deep freeze.

Leftovers are obviously better put away in the freezer if the alternative destination is several days lingering in the fridge and then the bin. On the other hand, beware against using the freezer as a less guilt-inducing way of binning food you know you don't want. If no one, including you, liked the soup the first time round (and that's why you've got so much left over) there is no point in freezing it for some hopeful future date when, miraculously, it will taste delicious. But bagging leftovers – say stews – in single portions can be useful for those evenings when you're eating alone. Take the little packet out of the deep-freeze before you go to work in the morning and heat it up for supper when you get back at night. Immensely cheering.

The freezer really comes into its own not so much when you don't have time for cooking as when you don't have time for shopping. In other words, the best use for the freezer is as a store cupboard.

As with a store cupboard, you must be on your guard against overstocking. In fact having far too much in the freezer can be very much worse than a mouldering store cupboard, because food so easily gets buried and really forgotten about rather than simply ignored. But a solid supply of ingredients with which to cook, rather than just wholly prepared dishes, can really help you make good simple things to eat without exhausting last-minute trawls around the supermarket.

You should always have in your freezer some raw prawns. Cooking with raw prawns rather than cooked ones makes such a difference, and the raw ones anyway seem to be sold only in their frozen state, so you just transplant them from the fishmonger's freezer to yours. You can cook them from frozen (which means you don't need to think about defrosting in advance) by plunging them, unthawed, into boiling water, salted and maybe spiked with a little vinegar. Peel them and pile them on top of garlicky puy lentils or mix them, cooled, into a fennel salad. When I was in Los Angeles some years back, I ate at Joachim Splichal's Patina the most wonderful starter of mashed potatoes and truffles with warm Santa Barbara shrimp on top. The combination works. Purée some potatoes (they need to be whipped as well as mashed) with butter and white pepper, put a small, or maybe not so small, mound on a plate, add some barely cooked prawns, then drizzle over some truffle oil if you have some, or some Liguarian olive oil if you haven't.

Bacon is another ingredient any cook should keep in store. (And I like to keep some pancetta there too.) I always freeze bacon in pairs of rashers, so that they defrost in minutes. The point about bacon is that everywhere, even the corner shop, sells it, but the good stuff is hard to find. I get my bacon from my butcher, and I know when I cook it that 1) white froth won't seep out of it, and 2) it will taste of bacon.

Nothing is as good as a bacon sandwich made with white bread. There are times when you just need to have that salty-sweet curl of seared flesh pressed between fat-softened, rind-stained spongy slices. My guiding rule is that I always have the wherewithal for a bacon sandwich in the house. I aim to keep all the ingredients for spaghetti carbonara to hand, too.

Bread is worth keeping in the freezer. It freezes well, and I keep good bread in loaves and plastic white bread (such as is needed for bacon sandwiches) in pairs of slices. It's when I have to go shopping for basics such as bread and milk that I come back having spent far too much on absolute unnecessities. Many varieties of milk now freeze all right, too: just check the labels first. For various reasons, all of them good ones, I try to keep visits to a supermarket to a minimum: I use my freezer to help keep me away.

You must keep stock in your freezer, and also the bones you have saved up to make it. Turn your freezer into your very own Golgotha, by throwing in lamb bones, chicken carcasses and any other bones that, these days, you are allowed to boil up. I have been known to take home the carcasses with me after a dinner party once I've found out that a) they have come from a butcher and b) they were going to be thrown away. Keep ham bones or leftover trimmings from gammon joints, too, to flavour pea and bean soups at some later date. It may make your freezer look like Dennis Nilsen's, but that is a small price to pay.

Freeze your own, consequent, home-made stock in manageable portions (see page 18). I also keep a couple of tubs of good fresh stock in my freezer. Certainly, fresh stock is very useful to have on hand: making a good fish fumet is rather more serious work than making a chicken stock, and I feel guiltless about having someone else do it for me, especially if it's done better than I would myself.

Parmesan rinds can be stowed away for future use. Every time you come to the end of a wedge of parmesan, or if you've left it out unwrapped for so long that it has become rebarbatively hard, don't throw the piece away, but chuck it in the freezer (preferably in a marked bag) to use whenever you make a minestrone or other soup which would benefit from that smoky, salty depth of flavouring.

As for puddings, other than the obvious ones that are meant to be frozen, such as ice-cream, you don't need to do more than keep a packet or so of frozen summer fruits, which can be made to serve in most eventualities. Remember that defrosted strawberries take on the texture of soft, cold slugs. Remove them from the packets of mixed fruits, and chuck them out.

If, like me, you're not much of a drinker, then you can stop yourself from wasting leftover wine after dinner parties by measuring out glassfuls and freezing them, well labelled (or you'll mistake white wine for egg whites, and see below), to use for cooking later on. And as for egg whites: I've got so many frozen, my freezer is beginning to look like a sperm bank.

Store Cupboard

UNLESS YOU WANT to spend your every waking free hour buying food, you need to have at home basic ingredients that you can use to make something good when you haven't had time to shop or plan for a particular meal. But don't believe what you are told about essentials: all it means is that you'll have a larder full of lost bottles of Indonesian soy sauce with a use-by date of November 1994. There is a compromise. Buy those few ingredients which really do provide a meal quickly and easily, and don't weigh yourself down with various tempting bits and pieces that you think you may get round to using one day.

I don't want to be too dictatorial, though. Apart from anything else, so much depends on the amount of space you've got. I am the Imelda Marcos – she who had a cushion with Nouveau Riche is Better than No Riche At All embroidered on it – of the foodshop world. I am not safe in delicatessens. No wonder I can't move for food I've bankrupted myself to buy. You have to avoid finding yourself in the same position. For there is no such thing as having food to cover most eventualities which doesn't also involve regularly throwing away food that goes off before you eat it.

It's not easy to hold back. Nothing is as good as buying food. Buying store-cupboard food is highly seductive: you don't have the stress of actual, imminent here-and-now cooking. It's fantasy shopping – and that's why it gets out of hand. Food bought on these expeditions lingers on for years, untouched. Partly this is because items you buy to store away are so often expensive, rarefied delicacies which, having bought, you then feel you have to save for something special. If you can get out of that frame of mind – which is the same mind-set that leads you to buy an extremely expensive piece of clothing which you then leave hanging in the wardrobe rather than allow it to be sullied by being worn around the house – then food shopping isn't quite such a dangerous pastime.

But it isn't the pattern of extravagance followed by austerity, nor the habit of saving things for best, which argues against intensive stockpiling. There is a hard-headed practical reason for being modest in your supplies: the food that people buy packets and packets of – flour, spices, rice, lentils – doesn't actually keep for ever. The chances are that you will end up with a larder full of stale pulses. It's not that this food goes off, necessarily, but it becomes less good to eat. It's comforting to know that you've got a bag of chick peas, but you must be strict with yourself and use it, not just keep it there for some rainy day when you fondly think you'll stay in and cook *pasta e ceci*. After a few years, they won't be dried, they'll be fossilised – and tasteless.

Anyway, unless you live in a very remote part of the country, the chances are that it won't be too difficult to go shopping for any special items you need for a specific recipe. A store cupboard is much more useful for keeping stuff in that you know you'll want regularly. This sort of food is likely to be the food you eat alone, or with your family. You want to be able to cook something in the evening after work without having to go shopping, and you don't want to have to start thinking about it before you get home. (I always want to think about what I'm going to eat, not in any elaborate organisational way, but because the speculation gives me pleasure. But there are many times when idly, greedily speculating is indeed the most energetic thing I can manage to do in advance. So what I need to know is that I have some food at home that won't take long to cook and won't demand too much of me.)

The most important ingredient to keep in your larder, or food cupboard, or whatever it might be, is pasta. Stick to a few different shapes only: if you try and cover too many bases, you will simply end up with about 10 opened, almost finished, packets and you will never be able to make a decent plateful of any of them. It's useful to have rather a lot of spaghetti, so that you can suddenly cook a huge plateful of something for a kitchen-load of people if need be. Linguine are sufficiently different to be worth having as well. Short pasta is quick and easier to cook for chidren; choose fusilli or penne, for example. Some kinds of eggy pasta need little cooking, and are therefore wonderful for when you feel like Elizabeth Taylor shouting 'Hurry!' to the microwave, as Joan Rivers' cruel joke had it.

I know I said that flour and so forth doesn't keep for ever, but I do keep a modest and restrained selection, including flours, especially Italian 00, sugars, salt, spices, oil, vinegar, tinned tomatoes, vanilla extract, stock cubes and vegetable stock powders. I also make up a jar of vanilla sugar – simply by filling a Kilner jar with caster sugar and chopping a couple of vanilla pods into about 5cm lengths to go in it. This takes very little effort, makes one feel positively holy and also gives one gloriously scented sugar to use in cakes, puddings, custards and so forth whenever needed. The pods give out their sweet and fleshy scent for ages; just pour over fresh sugar as you use it.

Naturally, what I want to keep in my kitchen cupboards might not be what you want to have in yours. But I couldn't live without Marsala, Noilly Prat (or Chambéry), dry sherry and sake pretty close to hand. I don't drink much, and so don't tend to have bottles of wine open; so if I need alcohol for cooking, I need to have it in the sort of bottles that come with a screw-top. Most often, I use Marsala in recipes which specify red wine, vermouth where white's required. Other drinks have their part to play: as ever, follow your own impulses; go with your own palate.

Any time I let myself run out of garlic or onions, I curse. The base-note ingredients should be a given in your kitchen, or you always feel you're scrabbling around before you can make *anything*. And for me, fresh nutmeg is crucial, too. You don't have to get a special little nutmeg grater (you could just shave off bits with a sharp knife) but it's not expensive, and it is useful.

Fridge

I KEEP A MODEST but restrained selection in my fridge, including butter, eggs, milk, salad leaves, some herbs and blocks of parmesan cheese. That's in theory; in reality it's a constant culinary clutter. I have either too much or not enough. But that's life.

Not everything in my kitchen is organic, but it seems to be going that way. Eggs, I've already mentioned: though make sure the box says organic and free-range as free-range alone doesn't signify anything very edifying. I want my meat free-range, traceable – the buzzword in organic farming – and not pumped full of revolting things. And now that supermarkets have got wise to the ever-more-widespread lure of organic produce it's easier to find vegetables from organic farms that aren't utterly covered in mud just to show their virtuous credentials. I worry about the chemicals in non-organic reared fruit and vegetables, but to tell the truth it's the improved taste of the organic stuff that's the clincher. If you can't muster the energy or interest to go wholly organic, just buy organic carrots. A few years back the government advised us to peel carrots because of the potentially harmful residues of chemicals which had been used in their cultivation. This is enough to make me feel that the real truth must be very much worse. Besides, organically grown carrots taste so much better. You should know that the difference in taste between organically and non-organically farmed potatoes is also pronounced. And it's worth buying organic oranges and lemons just because they're unwaxed and therefore better for zesting. But without the wax, they don't keep as long – there is a trade-off here – so just store them in the fridge if your turnover's slow.

Cooking in Advance

QUICK COOKING HAS become so implanted in people's minds as the way to eat well without having a nervous breakdown that everyone ignores the real way to make life easier for yourself: cooking in advance. Knocking up a meal in fifteen minutes is good for everyday cooking, when there's just one or two of you, or if you're one of those people who feels uncomfortable with too much planning. But when you're having people to dinner, life is made so much simpler if you don't have to do everything at the last minute. If you feel flustered at the very idea of cooking, indeed hate it, doing it in advance takes away some of the stress: if you enjoy it, you'll enjoy it more if you don't put yourself under pressure; that's for the professionals, who thrive on it. I love the feeling of pottering about the kitchen, cooking slowly, stirring and chopping and getting everything done when I'm feeling well-disposed and not utterly exhausted. When I cook with too much of an audience I immediately worry about what'll happen if something goes wrong, and then, of course, something does.

Cook in advance and, if the worst comes to the worst, you can ditch it. No one but you will know that it tasted disgusting, or failed to set, or curdled or whatever. That may sound a rather negative approach, but in fact it's liberating; moreover, because you're not stressed out or desperately working against the clock, there's less chance of disaster. And if something does go wrong, you have the time calmly to find a way of rectifying it.

And things do go wrong in cooking. Indeed, it's one of the ways you learn and eventually find your own style. Some of the best food I've cooked has been as a result of trying to make up for some fault, some blip. It's when you're exploring and trying out, not simply following a recipe, that you feel what the food needs, what will make it taste how you want it to taste. Without the pressure of having to perform, you can concentrate on the food. This is not to say that cooking has to be a solitary pursuit. In a way, there's nothing better than cooking with someone to talk to while you do it. But I am someone who panics if there's too much commotion or if I've got too little time to think.

Perhaps this is a temperamental thing, but cooking is about temperament, and so, I think, is eating. You have to find a way of cooking that suits you, and that isn't just about your life, your working hours, your environment, though these, of course, matter. But what counts, too, is whether you're the sort of person who's soothed or cramped by list-making, whether you're impatient or tidy, whether spontaneity makes you feel creative or panic-stricken. Most of us like eating, but many people feel flustered and a sense of panic and, frankly, boredom when it comes to cooking. It's difficult to be good at something you aren't really interested in. But some people don't like cooking simply because they've never given themselves the chance to do it calmly and quietly and in the right mood. Obligation can be a useful prompt to activity, but it can be a terrible blight, too. Cooking in advance is a good way to learn confidence, to learn what works and why and how, and from that you can then teach yourself to trust your intuition, to be spontaneous: in short, to cook.

Cooking is about working towards a goal, towards something you have decided upon in advance. But any creative work (however cringe-makingly pretentious it sounds, cooking *is* creative, has to be) needs to liberate itself from the end product during the act of producing. This can be very difficult. There are practical constraints, which are what make the form, in cooking as in poetry. You have to learn to use these constraints to your advantage. Get over economic constraints by buying ingredients you can afford rather than making do with inferior versions of expensive produce. Make the best of the equipment you happen to have in your kitchen. Be rcady to adapt to what you've got. But some other constraints – such as lack of time – merely add to your obstacles, and to the risk that if your dinner is inedible you and your guests will just have to live with it.

Some food actually benefits from being cooked in advance. Stews, for example, are always best cooked, left to get cold and hang around for a while, and then reheated. Puddings can need time to set or for their flavours to settle and deepen. Soups mellow. That's why I love this sort of cooking: the rhythms are so reassuring; I no longer feel I'm snatching at food, at life. It's not exactly that I'm constructing a domestic idyll, but as I work in the kitchen at night, or at the weekend, filling the house with the smells of baking and roasting and filling the fridge with good things to eat, it feels, corny as it sounds, as if I'm making a home.

Soup

Soups are the obvious place to start for those thus in domestic goddess mode. Soups, of course, are some of the quickest meals that you can make. Somehow the home-made soup, lovingly prepared in advance, is no longer popular. I think it comes down to stock: our disinclination to make it from scratch, together with our disdain for cubes. It is important to stress that even though the better a stock the better a soup, it does not follow that no good soup, no superlatively good soup, can be made with stock cubes. Naturally, it depends on the kind of soup: no consommé or delicate broth should be made with anything but home-made stock; but a hearty vegetable soup can, frankly, be made with water; and in between these two extremes, use stock cubes.

If you haven't already got a supply of home-made stock in the freezer, you'll need a good day's grace: time to make the stock, to cool it, to skim the fat off it. A ham stock (just the liquid in which a gammon's been cooked) makes all the difference to a pea soup; a chicken stock, light though it may be, gives instant depth and velvety swell to a very basic parsnip soup. Grate fresh parmesan over the pea soup; drop chilli oil into the pale sweetness of the parsnip to add a probing fierceness. To both you could add some bacon, fried, grilled or baked in a hot oven, and crumbled into salty shards; marjoram, too, would work equally well with either.

This soup can be made in advance and kept in the fridge for reheating throughout the week, whether on the hob or in the microwave.

The soups that you really have to cook in advance are the ones made from pulses. Most legumes need a good day's soaking. I tend to put beans into soak as I go to bed even if I won't actually be cooking with them until the next evening. Chick peas need 24 hours, and I don't mind if I give them 36. And they need a lot of cooking, much longer than you are usually told. There seems to be a conspiracy to misinform you about chick peas: I cannot believe the number of times I've read that 45 minutes will do, when it takes double that time to cook them. Anna Del Conte is realistic about this, admitting that some chick peas can take as long as 4 hours. I use her technique for preparing chick peas. Put them in a bowl and cover them with cold water. Then mix together 1 teaspoon bicarbonate of soda and 1 tablespoon each of salt and flour – or those ingredients in that ratio: a very large quantity of peas will need more of this tenderising mixture – add water to form a runny paste and stir this paste into the soaking chick peas. Leave for a good 24 hours. Then, when cooking the chick peas (drained and rinsed), don't lift the lid off the pan for the first hour or so or the peas will harden. (Curiosity often gets the better of me.) Broad beans similarly need longer soaking than, say, cannellini or borlotti (both of which are fine with 12 hours), and all are better if you leave the salting till the last moments of the cooking time. If you're cooking in advance, it doesn't matter how long it all takes: and good though canned chick peas are, dried, soaked and cooked ones are so much better. You can taste the full, grainy, chestnutty roundness of them.

Chick pea and pasta soup is my favourite soup of all. You can cook it days before you actually want to eat it. Obviously it can't all be done in advance because the pasta must be cooked at the last minute, but since you have to reheat the soup anyway, what does it matter to you if, when reheating, you keep it simmering for 20 minutes or so extra while the ditalini swell and soften.

I cook this soup so often – just for us, at home, for

supper, in great big greedy bowlfuls; for a first course when I've got people coming for dinner; or, if they're coming for a Saturday lunch, for a main course, with a salad and cheese after – that I don't follow a recipe any more. But this is the recipe that started me off. It is Anna Del Conte's, adapted from her *Entertaining all'Italiana*. I have several copies of this book: one in the kitchen, where, eccentrically perhaps, I tend not to keep my cookery books; one in my study, where all books on food notionally live (in practice they are dotted on floors, in lavatories, throughout the house); and one in the bedroom, for late-night soothing reading and midnight-feast fantasising.

Anna's chick pea and pasta soup

This will make enough soup for 8. I sometimes add a glass of white wine or any stock to hand, from whatever animal it emanates, but the soup has quite enough taste with simply water. If you want a vegetable stock, choose a low-salt bouillon powder. You can make the soup (bar the pasta) up to 3 days in advance, or longer if you want to freeze it.

400g dried chick peas
2 teaspoons bicarbonate of soda
2 tablespoons flour
2 tablespoons salt
3 litres vegetable stock (or meat stock or white wine and water)
3 sprigs rosemary

8 cloves garlic, peeled and bruised
120ml extra virgin olive oil
400g fresh tomatoes, skinned and seeded
270g small tubular pasta such as ditalini
parmesan for grating over
chilli oil and flat-leaf parsley if you want

Put the chick peas in a bowl and cover with plenty of water. Mix together the bicarbonate of soda, flour and salt and add enough water to make a thin paste. Stir this mixture into the bowl with the chick peas and leave to soak for at least 12 hours, preferably 24.

When the chick peas have doubled their size (you don't have to get your ruler out: trust your eyes) they are ready to be cooked. Drain and then rinse them. Put them in a large pot and add the vegetable stock, meat stock or white wine and water or the same quantity of water.

Tie the rosemary sprigs in a muslin bag and add to the pot. This will make it possible to remove the rosemary without leaving any needles to float in the soup. This might sound pernickety, but when I ignored the advice I found the sharp and, by now, bitter needles an unpleasant intrusion. If you feel intimidated by the idea of muslin then use, disgusting though it sounds, a popsock or stocking and tie a knot at the open end, or a tea-infuser. Frankly, it doesn't matter what you use providing it does the job, although I imagine untreated muslin is better. You can get muslin or cheesecloth in any kitchen shop or haberdashery department and, come to think of it, in a baby department selling muslin napkins; one of those posset-catching squares you wear over your shoulder to catch infant regurgitations would do.

Add the garlic and pour in half the oil. Cover the pan tightly and bring to the boil. You will have to gauge this by ear without peeping in. Lower the heat and cook over the lowest simmer until the chick peas are tender, which can take 2–4 hours. Take a look after 1½ hours. Do not add any salt until the chick peas are nearly ready. If you put it in too soon, they'll harden.

When the chick peas are tender, remove the garlic and the rosemary bundle, which should be floating on the surface. Purée the tomatoes through a food mill or in a food processor and add to the soup with their juice. Stir well, add salt and pepper to taste and cook for a further 10 minutes or so. This is the point at which you should stop when you're cooking the soup in advance.

When you want to eat it, put it back on the hob and reheat it, so that you can proceed to the final step, which is to cook the pasta. Before you add the pasta, check that there is enough liquid in the pan. You may have to add some boiling water. Now, to the boiling soup, add the pasta and cook till al dente. I like to add some freshly chopped flat-leaf parsley, but the glory of this soup will be undiminished if you prefer not to. But do pour some of the remaining oil into the pot of soup, and drizzle some more into each bowl after you've ladled the soup in. Or just pour some into the big pot and let people add what they want as they eat. I would put good extra virgin olive oil on the table as well as a bottle of chilli oil for those who like some heat: and it does work. Serve, too, the parmesan, put on a plate with a grater, so people can add their own.

Kafka-esque or soft and crispy duck

You'd think, wouldn't you, that a roast could never ever be done in advance. Yes, we all know that any joint needs to rest after it's come out of the oven and before it goes on the table, but I now do a roast duck – the best roast duck I have ever eaten, let alone cooked – that can be started a good few days before you want to eat it. This is semi-cooking in advance and I'm blazingly evangelical about it. A method of doing the perfect roast duck which leaves you with just three-quarters of an hour's cooking on the night – and all in the oven, no basting, no faffing, nothing – has to be a good thing. I let the duck sit around in the fridge in a state of semi-cookedness for up to 3 days; but if you feel at all nervous about this, don't leave it as long. But actually, before we get on to it, it isn't that new an idea: Apicius – he of the first cookery book – likewise instructed his readers: 'lavas, ornas et in olla elixabis cum aqua, sale et aneto dimidia coctura'. Admittedly, even if he suggested boiling the duck in water (with dill as well as salt) until half-cooked, the second half's cooking would not be exactly by roasting; it would have been more like pot-roasting. Nevertheless, it reminds us pointedly that there is nothing new in cooking. That's if it's to taste good.

But this is the story: when I was last in New York I bought a copy of Barbara Kafka's *Roasting*, the premise of which is that roasting at very high temperatures makes for the most succulent, fleshily yielding and crispy skinned birds and joints. The drawback is that you need a clean oven, otherwise all that roasting at very high temperatures gives you a smoky kitchen, burning eyes and an acrid glaze on the putative pièce de résistance. I noticed that there was a recipe for roast duck which involved poaching the bird first in stock for about three-quarters of an hour and then blitzing it in the oven for half an hour. The result: tender flesh and crisp skin. And it's true, if you're not careful when you roast a duck in the more usual way you often find that the desirably crunchy carapace comes at the cost of overcooked and thus stringy meat. Everyone has an answer to this one: covering the bird with boiling water, hanging it up on a clothes line on a blustery (but dry) day, suspending it on high by means of a clothes hanger then getting a stiff wrist by aiming a hair-dryer, at full though icy blast, at it for hours.

The *echt* Kafka-esque technique involves poaching the duck, upright, in a thin, tall pot in duck stock. I couldn't quite see why you needed to poach the bird in stock, since the flesh is rich itself. More to the point, I had none. So the first time I tried it, I put the water into the requisite tall thin pot (the bottom half of my couscoussier), added the giblets, brought it to the boil, added salt, and lowered in the duck. Then, as directed, I made sure the bird was submerged for the whole 40 minutes. I did this in the morning, let the duck get cool, put it in the fridge and then brought it out in the evening, letting it get to room temperature before roasting it for thc 30 minutes as recommended.

The next time I tried it, I made some changes. For one

thing, duck doesn't yield much flesh, and cooking a single, lone, duck is no use unless there are only 2 or 3 of you eating. But I couldn't get 2 ducks into my couscoussier, and getting even one out, from an upright position, tore its skin. So I decided to be even more disobedient. Figuring that the ducks would stay moist if they were steamed, not necessarily submerged, I put one duck, breast down, in a large, oblong casserole and the other in a large, deep, all-purpose frying pan. Both pans were filled with boiling salted water. The casserole had its own lid, and for the frying pan I made a tent of tin foil. I wasn't sure it would work, but there's only ever one way of finding out.

I had decided anyway – on the evidence produced by my first stab – to swap around cooking times: that's to say, poach the birds for the ½ hour and roast them for ¾ hour. The ducks weren't exactly the same size (one was about 1½ kg, the other perhaps 300g heavier) but I didn't alter the poaching times to suit: I merely took the lighter one out of its water first. And it is very much easier taking the ducks out when they are flat rather than upright. Use wooden paddle-spoons or rubber spatulas to make sure you don't rip the flesh. It would be even easier to steam the birds breast up, and frankly I doubt it matters which way up they are. I noticed some slight scalding to a patch on both ducks where the breast had come into contact with the hot base of the pan, but this didn't seem to make any difference either.

Boiling ducks produces a rather pongy fug which can

linger in the kitchen, so open a window; but I was going away for the weekend and had promised to cook something. I knew I wouldn't have time to poach the birds on the Friday so did them on Thursday at about six in the evening, let them cool on a baking tray with a wire-mesh grill arrangement set over it, and then put them in the fridge before going to bed.

For travelling on Friday evening I just put them in a plastic bag and put that plastic bag in a picnic coolbag. On arrival, I put the ducks, uncovered, on a large plate in my friends' fridge. When I got around to cooking them – which turned out to be Sunday lunch – it transpired that their Aga had died. I put the birds, anyway, into the supposedly hot oven, which turned out to be a rapidly cooling sooty box, and left them there for a hopeless 20 minutes. The ducks just got greasy, not even hot, and I got more teary and mutinous by the minute. But someone living in a neighbouring farm set her oven to high for me (she was doubtful about having ducks at top whack so we compromised on gas mark 8/220°C): the ducks were driven over to her, roasted for 45 minutes and came back, after the brief car journey, bronze and crisp and perfect.

I don't think it is possible to try out a recipe more conclusively than that.

I LOVE HAVING someone in the kitchen just to talk to as I chop, and weigh, and stir, and generally get things ready. I love cooking with other people, too. I do it rarely, though

I love having someone in the kitchen just to talk to as I chop, and weigh, and stir, and generally get things ready

used to often with my sister Thomasina. There's something about that industrious intimacy that is both cushioning and comforting, but also hugely confidence-building. I love that sense of companionable bustle, of linked activity and joint enterprise. It makes it easier to attempt food that normally you would shrink from, not because you rely on another's superior capabilities or experience necessarily, but because you aren't isolated in the attempt. Everything doesn't feel geared towards the end product because it is a shared activity – and that itself is pleasurable. You feel a sense of satisfaction about the process. It isn't drudgery.

Claudia Roden, writing about her memories of childhood in Egypt, recollected kitchenfuls of women kneading and pummelling pastries, stuffing them, wrapping them, baking them together. But I suppose those Middle Eastern delicacies, meticulous confections with their elaborate *farces*, could have sprung only from a culture in which the cooking was carried out by posses, by armies, of sisters and female relatives. It doesn't do to get too lyrical about this culinary companionship, though: which of us now would want our lives to be spent in such service, companionable though it might have been?

Still, it's a pity to lose all of it, never to become immersed in that female kitchen bustle. For me, so much of cooking in advance is tied up with that image, that idea: that's when cooking feels like the making of provisions, the bolstering up of a life. I don't see it as a form of subjection (unless the position is a forced one) and I don't see it as a secondary role, either. Some people hate domesticity, I know. I'm glad I don't: I love the absorbing satisfactions of the kitchen. For me, the pleasure to be got from cooking, from food – in the shop, on the chopping board, on the plate or in the pan – is aesthetic. I think it's that I find food beautiful, intensely so.

Proper English trifle

When I say proper I mean proper: lots of sponge, lots of jam, lots of custard and lots of cream. This is not a timid construction, nor should it be. Of course, the ingredients must be good, but you don't want to end up with a trifle so upmarket it's inappropriately, posturingly elegant. A degree of vulgarity is requisite.

I soak the sponge in orange-flavoured alcohol (I loathe the acrid dustiness of standard-issue sherry), infuse the custard with orange, and make an orange caramel to sprinkle over the top; this seems to bring out the fruity, egginess of it all, even if you are reduced to using frozen fruit. I've specified raspberries but you could substitute blackberries (maybe sprinkling with a little sugar and using blackberry jam with the sponge), and I have used, too, those packets of frozen mixed berries. They're fine, but they definitely bring a sponge-sousing reminder of summer pudding with them. You can use trifle sponges here, and I do, but for those who cannot countenance such an un-chic thing, I suggest some brioche or challah, sliced; indeed, loaf-shaped supermarket brioche or challah, which have a denser crumb than the boulangerie-edition or *echt* article, are both perfect here.

In a way it is meaningless, or certainly unhelpful, to give exact measurements; as ever it so depends on the bowl you're using. Think rather of layers: one of jam-sandwiched sponge, one of custard, one of cream, and then the nutty, toffee-ish topping. So use the quantities below – which will fill a bowl of about 1½ litre capacity – as a guide only.

600ml single cream
zest and juice of 1 orange
100ml Grand Marnier
50ml Marsala
5 trifle sponges or 4–5 slices of brioche or challah
approx. 10 heaped teaspoons best quality raspberry or boysonberry jam
500g raspberries
8 egg yolks
75g caster sugar
450ml double cream
50g flaked almonds
1 orange
approx. 100g sugar

Pour the single cream into a wide, heavy-based saucepan, add the orange zest – reserving the juice, separately, for the moment – and bring to the boil without actually letting it boil. Take off the heat and set aside for the orange flavour to infuse while you get on with the bottom layer of the trifle.

Mix together the Grand Marnier, Marsala and the reserved orange juice and pour about half of it into a shallow soup bowl, keeping the rest for replenishing halfway through. If you're using the trifle sponges, split them horizontally, if the challah or brioche slices, take the crusts off and cut them each into two equal slices. Make little sandwiches with the jam, and dunk each sandwich, first one side, then the other, into the booze in the bowl and then arrange the alcohol-sodden sandwiches at the bottom of the trifle bowl. If you're using the challah or brioche, you might need to make up more of your alcoholic mixture, as the bread seems to soak it all in much more quickly and thirstily.

When the bottom of the bowl's covered, top with the fruit and put in the fridge to settle while you get on with the custard. Bring the orange-zested cream back to the boil, while you whisk together the egg yolks and sugar in a bowl large enough to take the cream, too, in a moment. When the yolks and sugar are thick and frothy, pour the about-to-bubble cream into them, whisking as you do so. Wash out the pan, dry it well and return the custard mixture, making sure you disentangle every whisk-attached string of orange zest; you will be sieving later, but for now you want to hold on to all of it.

Fill the sink with enough cold water to come about halfway up the custard pan. On medium to low heat cook the custard, stirring all the time with a wooden spoon or spatula. With so many egg yolks, the custard should take hardly any time to thicken (and remember it will continue to thicken further as it cools) so don't overcook it. If it looks as if it might be about to boil or split, quickly plunge the pan into the sink of cold water, beating furiously until danger is averted. But I find this yolk-rich custard uneventful to make: about 7 minutes, if that, does it; it's unlikely to need cooking for more than 10. When it's cooked and thickened, take the pan over to the sink of cold water and beat robustly but calmly for a minute or so. When the custard's smooth and cooled, strain it over the fruit-topped sponge and put the bowl back in the fridge for 24 hours.

Not long before you want to eat it, whip the double cream till thick and, preferably with one of those bendy rubber spatulas, smear it thickly over the top of the custard. Put it back in the fridge. Toast the flaked almonds by tossing them in a hot, dry frying pan for a couple of minutes and then remove to a plate till cool. Squeeze the orange, pour it into a measuring jug and then measure out an equal quantity – gram for millilitre – of sugar; I reckon on getting 100ml of juice out of the average orange. Pour the orange juice into a saucepan and stir in sugar to help it dissolve. Bring to the boil and let bubble away until you have a thick but still runny toffee: if you let it boil too much until you have, almost, toffee (and I often do) it's not the end of the world, but you're aiming for a densely syrupy, sticky caramel. Remove from heat, and when cooled slightly, dribble over the whipped cream; you may find this easier to do teaspoon by slow-drizzling teaspoon. You can do this an hour or so before you want to eat it. Scatter the toasted almonds over before serving.

This is certainly enough for 10, and maybe even more, though it certainly wouldn't swamp 8.

One & Two

'DON'T KNOCK MASTURBATION,' Woody Allen once said: 'it's sex with someone I love.' Most people can't help finding something embarrassingly onanistic about taking pleasure in eating alone. Even those who claim to love food think that cooking just for yourself is either extravagantly self-indulgent or a plain waste of time and effort. But you don't have to belong to the drearily narcissistic learn-to-love-yourself school of thought to grasp that it might be a good thing to consider yourself worth cooking for. And the sort of food you cook for yourself will be different from the food you might lay on for tablefuls of people: it will be better.

I don't say that for effect. You'll feel less nervous about cooking it and that translates to the food itself. It'll be simpler, more straightforward, the sort of food *you* want to eat.

I don't deny that food, its preparation as much as its consumption, is about sharing, about connectedness. But that's not all that it's about. There seems to me to be something robustly affirmative about taking trouble to feed yourself; enjoying life on purpose, rather than by default.

Even in culinary terms alone there are grounds for satisfaction. Real cooking, if it is to have any authenticity, any integrity, has to be part of how you are, a function of your personality, your temperament. There's too much culinary ventriloquism about as it is: cooking for yourself is a way of countering that. It's how you're going to find your own voice. One of the greatest hindrances to enjoying cooking is that tense-necked desire to impress others. It's virtually impossible to be innocent of this. Even if this is not your motivation, it's hard, if you're being honest, to be insensible to the reactions of others. Since cooking for other people is about trying to please them, it would be strange to be indifferent to their pleasure, and I don't think you should be. But you can try too hard. When you're cooking for yourself, the stakes simply aren't as high. You don't mind as much. Consequently, it's much less likely to go wrong. And the process is more enjoyable in itself.

When I cook for myself I find it easier to trust my instinct – I am sufficiently relaxed to listen to it in the first place – and, contrariwise, I feel freer to overturn a judgement, to take a risk. If I want to see what will happen if I add yoghurt, or stir in some chopped tarragon instead of parsley, I can do so without worrying that I am about to ruin everything. If the sauce splits or the tarragon infuses everything with an invasive farmyard grassiness, I can live with it. I might feel cross with myself, but I won't be panicked. It could be that the yoghurt makes the sauce, or that the tarragon revitalises it. I'm not saying that cooking for seven other people would make it impossible for me to respond spontaneously, but I do think it's cooking for myself that has made it possible.

Far too much cooking now is about the tyranny of the recipe on the one hand and the absence of slowly acquired experience on the other. Cooking for yourself is a way of finding out what *you* want to cook and eat, rather than simply joining up the dots. Crucially, it's a way of seeing which things work, which don't, and how ingredients, heat, implements, vessels, all have their part to play. When I feel like a bowl of thick, jellied white rice noodles, not soupy but barely bound in a sweet and salty sauce, I'm not going to look up a recipe for them. I know that if I soak the noodles in boiling water until they dislodge themselves from the solid wodge I've bought them in, fry 2 cloves of garlic with some knife-flattened spring onions and tiny square beads of chopped red chilli in a pan before wilting some greens and adding the noodles with a steam-provoking gush of soy and mirin, with maybe a teaspoon of black bean sauce grittily dissolved in it, it will taste wonderful, comforting, with or without chopped coriander or a slow-oozing drop or two of sesame oil. I can pay attention to texture and to taste. I know what sort of thing I'm going to end up with, but I'm not aiming to replicate any particular dish. Sometimes it goes wrong: I'm too heavy-handed with the soy and drench everything in brown brine, so that the sweet stickiness of the rice sticks is done for, and there's no contrast; I might feel, when eating, that the chilli interrupts too much when I'm in the mood to eat something altogether gentler. These aren't tragedies, however. And frankly most often I get satisfaction simply from the quiet putting together of a meal. It calms me, which in turn makes me enjoy eating it more.

But cooking for yourself isn't simply therapy and training. It also happens to be a pleasure in itself. Since most women don't have lives now whereby we're plunged into three family meals a day from the age of nineteen, we're not forced to learn how to cook from the ground up. I don't complain. Nor do I wish to make it sound as if cooking for yourself were some sort of checklisted culinary foundation course. The reason why you learn so much from the sort of food you casually throw together for yourself, is that you're learning by accident, by osmosis. This has nothing to do with the culinary supremacism of the great chefs, or those who'd ape them. Too many people cook only when they're giving a dinner party. And it's very hard to go from nought to a hundred miles an hour. How can you learn to feel at ease around food, relaxed about cooking, if every time you go into the kitchen it's to cook at competition level?

I love the open-ended freedom of just pottering about

in the kitchen, of opening the fridge door and deciding what to cook. But I like, too, the smaller special project, the sort of indulgent eating that has something almost ceremonial about it when done alone. I'm not saying I don't often end up with that au pair special, a bowl of cereal, or its street-princess equivalent, the phone-in pizza. But I believe in the rule of 'Tonight Lucullus is dining with Lucullus.'

EATING ALONE, FOR me, is most often a prompt to shop. This is where self-absorption and consumerism meet: a rapt, satisfyingly convoluted pleasure. The food I want most to buy is the food I most often try not to eat: a swollen-bellied tranche of cheese, a loaf of bread. These constitute the perfect meal. A slither of gorgonzola or coulommiers sacrificed on the intrusive and unyielding surface of a Bath Oliver at the end of dinner is food out of kilter. Just bread and cheese is fine to give others if you've shown the consideration of providing variety. But I want for myself the obsessive focus of the one huge, heady *baveuse* soft cheese, or else a wedge of the palate-burning hard stuff: too much, too strong. If I'm eating a salty blue cheese, its texture somewhere between creamy and crumbly, I want baguette or a bitter, fudge-coloured *pain au levain*; with cheddar, real cheddar, I want doughier English white bread: whichever, it must be a whole loaf. I might eat tomatoes with the bread and cheese, but the tomatoes mustn't be in a salad, but left whole on the plate, to be sliced or chopped, *à la minute*. But, then, I love the delicatessen-garnered equivalent of the TV supper.

I am pretty keen on the culinary ethos of the Greasy Spoon, too: bacon sandwiches, fried-egg sandwiches, egg *and* bacon sandwiches, sausage sandwiches; none requires much in the way of attention, and certainly nothing in the way of expertise. Even easier is a sandwich that on paper sounds fancier, a fab merging of caff and deli culture: get a large flat field mushroom, put it in a preheated gas mark 6/200°C oven covered with butter, chopped garlic and parsley for about 20 minutes; when ready, and garlicky, buttery juices are oozing with black, cut open a soft roll, small ciabatta or bap, or chunk of baguette even, and wipe the cut side all over the pan to soak up the pungent juices. Smear with Dijon mustard, top with the mushroom, squeeze with lemon juice, sprinkle some salt and add some chopped lettuce or parsley as you like; think of this as a fungoid – but strangely hardly less meaty – version of steak sandwich. Bite in, with the juices dripping down your arm as you eat.

There are other memorable more or less non-cooking solitary suppers: one is a bowl of Heinz tomato soup with some pale, undercooked but overbuttered toast (crusts off for full nostalgic effect); another, microwave-zapped, mustard-dunked frankfurters (proper frankfurters, from a delicatessen, not those flabby, mousse-textured things out of a tin). The difficulty is that if I have them in the house, I end up eating them while I wait for whatever I'm actually cooking for dinner to be ready. And my portions are not small to start off with. Two defences, other than pure greed: I hate meagreness, the scant, sensible serving; and if I long to eat a particular thing, I want lots of it. I don't want course upon course, and I don't want excess every day. But when it comes to a feast, I don't know the meaning of enough.

Cooking for two is just an amplification of cooking for one (rather than the former being a diminution of the latter). To tell the truth, with my cooking and portion-size, there isn't often a lot to choose between them. Many of the impulses that inform or inspire this sort of cooking are the same: the desire to eat food that is relaxed but at times culinarily elevated without loss of spontaneity; the pleasures of fiddling about with what happens to be in the fridge; and, as with any form of eating, the need to make food part of the civilised context in which we live.

Linguine with clams

My absolutely favourite dinner to cook for myself is linguine with clams. I have a purely personal reason for thinking of fish, of any sort, as the ideal solitary food because I live with someone who's allergic to it. But my principle has wider application: fish doesn't take long to cook and tastes best dealt with simply, but because it has to be bought fresh needs enough planning to have something of the ceremonial about it. I don't know why spaghetti alle vongole (I use linguine because I prefer, here, the more substantial, more resistant and at the same time more sauce-absorbent tangle they make in the mouth) is thought of as restaurant food, especially since most restaurants in this country ruin it by adding tomatoes. I have to have my sauce *bianco*.

The whole dish is easy to make. It is, for me, along with a steak béarnaise, unchallengeable contender for that great, fantasy Last Meal on Earth.

You can use venus clams, but palourdes or vongole are what you're after; at a good fishmonger's, you shouldn't have any trouble finding them. If you've got venus clams, add 1 tablespoon of bicarbonate of soda to the soaking water. If you've got the bigger palourdes, you may not need to soak them at all, a brisk wash may be enough: ask your fishmonger.

200g clams
150g linguine
1 clove garlic
2 tablespoons olive oil
½ dried red chilli pepper
80ml white wine or vermouth (Noilly Prat)
1–2 tablespoons fresh parsley, chopped

Put the clams to soak in a sinkful of cold water, if necessary, while you heat the water for the pasta. When the water comes to the boil, add salt and then the linguine. Cook the linguine until nearly but not quite ready: you're going to give them a fractional amount more cooking with the clams and their winey juices. Try and time this so that the pasta's ready at the time you want to plunge it into the clams. Otherwise drain and douse with a few drops of olive oil.

Mince or finely slice the garlic and, in a pan with a lid into which you can fit the pasta later, fry it gently (it mustn't burn) in the olive oil and then crumble in the red chilli pepper. Drain the clams, discarding those that remain open, and add them to the garlic pan. Pour over the wine or vermouth and cover. In 2 minutes, the clams should be open. Add the pasta, put the lid on again and swirl about. In another minute or so everything should have finished cooking and come together: the pasta will have cooked to the requisite tough tenderness and absorbed the salty, garlicky winey clam juices, and be bound in a wonderful almost-pungent sea-syrup. But if the pasta needs more cooking, clamp on the lid and give it more time. Chuck out any clams which have failed to open.

Add half the parsley, shake the pan to distribute evenly, and turn onto a plate or into a bowl and sprinkle over the rest of the parsley. Cheese is not grated over any pasta with fish in it in Italy (nor indeed where garlic is the predominant ingredient, either) and the rule holds good. You need add nothing. It's perfect already.

THE ESSENCE OF eating for two exists in just one word: steak. I'm not saying I wouldn't cook it just for me, but there's something solid, old-fashioned and comforting about the two of you sitting down and eating steak. Too often when I'm at home alone I waft along, as you do, in a tangle of noodles, lemon grass and suchlike. Steak béarnaise is my dream. Fry a steak as a steak is fried, on a hot pan and for a short time. I don't do frites. Green salad made bloody with the steak's juices, and some real baguette, more than make up, in my book, for my chip deficiency; but then I live practically next door to a chip shop, so if I'm eating with someone who takes a less tolerant line, I'm safe. Just as I think that roast chicken is so good that I need a lot of persuading to cook it any other way, so I feel about steak that it is perfect simply grilled or fried. But steak au poivre, aux poivres, peppered steak, whichever handle you like to put on it, is, in shorn form, a forceful contender. For me it's better without the addition of cream; I like my steak butch, brown and meaty. This is hardly the orthodox approach, and I can see that you might feel a culinary classic ought to be respected. Sometimes I'd even agree. Just go cautiously. You don't want to feel you're having pudding at the same time.

Steak au poivre

I use either black peppercorns, half black, half white or, more often, a many-berried pepper mixture: some of the mixture isn't strictly speaking pepper at all, but I like its warm aromatic quality, rather mellower than the heat of pepper alone. I have been meaning for years now to buy a coffee grinder especially for spices, but still haven't managed to do so and use a pestle and mortar.

2 middle-cut rump steaks (or sirloin if you prefer), about 3cm thick
scant tablespoon olive oil
3 tablespoons peppercorns, ground coarsely (see above)
3 tablespoons butter, plus more if liked
3 tablespoons brandy

Using a pastry brush if you've got one, paint the steaks on both sides with oil; you should need not more than a teaspoon on each side. Then dredge the oily steaks in the mashed peppercorns: you want a good crusty coat. If the corns are too coarse, they'll just fall off; if they're too fine, you won't stop coughing when you eat them.

In a heavy-bottomed pan, put the remaining oil to heat up. Add the steaks, and sear on each side, then, over moderate heat, add the butter and another drop of olive oil and cook the steaks for about another 3 minutes a side or to requisite bloodiness. Remove to warmed plates. Turn the heat up to high again, then pour in the brandy, stirring well all the time to deglaze the pan. When you've got a thick syrupy glaze, taste it: you may want to add salt, and you may want to whisk in a little butter just to help it all taste and look smooth and amalgamated. This, too, is where you could add your dollop of cream if you wanted. I've also, instead of the brandy, used Marsala, without which I'm pathologically incapable of existing, and it was dee-licious.

Serves 2.

EVERY DAY I thank God, or his supermarket stand-in, for frozen peas. For me, they are a leading ingredient, a green meat, almost. I don't eat them that much, straight, as a vegetable, but I'd hate to have to cook without them. The almost instant soup – a handful of peas, a jugful of stock, a rind of cheese, whatever's to hand – makes for a sweetly restoring supper. The pea risotto that follows is another regular. Risotto is best suited to two. I like relative peace in which to cook it, and I prefer handling small quantities. It is also the world's best comfort food.

The quantities I use might be nearer those ordinarily specified for four; but when I cook risotto I don't want to eat anything else after. And I feel a pang if there's only enough for one middling-sized flat puddle of the stuff.

Pea risotto

I specify frozen petits pois, simply because that's what I always use. I have used real peas, just podded, to make *risi e bisi*, the fabulously named Venetian slurpily soft risotto, or thick rice soup, however you like to think of it, complete with pea-pod stock. But to be frank, if you don't grow peas yourself, then there is (as I may have mentioned, and I do, often) not a huge advantage in using fresh ones. By the time they're in the shops, they're big and starchy and without that extraordinary, almost floral, scent; that heady but contained sweetness of peas just picked from the garden.

On the whole, I take the peas out and let them thaw before using them. But I don't see that it makes much difference.

Every day I thank God, or his supermarket stand-in, for frozen peas

As for stock: I haven't specified any in particular. When I can, I use ham stock which, because of my stock-making obsession, I usually have in the freezer; otherwise I make up some with vegetable stock granules. I wouldn't use a dark beef stock here, but any chicken, veal or light broth would be fine.

60g butter
150g frozen petits pois
approx. 1 litre stock
2 tablespoons freshly grated parmesan, plus more for the table
grated nutmeg
1 small onion or, even better, banana shallot
drop of oil
200g arborio or Canaroli rice
80ml white wine or vermouth

Put about a third of the butter in a pan and when it's melted add the peas, and cook, stirring every now and again, for 2 minutes. Remove half the peas and to the remaining half in the pan add a ladleful of the stock. Put a lid on the pan and let cook gently for about 5 minutes or so till soft. Purée this mixture – I use the mini electric chopper I used to use for baby food – with 1 tablespoon each of grated parmesan and butter and a grating each of pepper and fresh nutmeg.

Meanwhile, chop the onion or shallot very finely, and melt another tablespoon of butter, with a drop of oil in it, in a pan. Cook the onion, stirring with your wooden prodder, for about 4 minutes, then add the rice and stir till every grain glistens with the oniony fat. Pour in the wine or vermouth (last time I did this

I used Chambéry and it was fabulous: it seemed to add to the grassy freshness of the peas) and let it bubble away and absorb. Then add a ladleful of the hot stock (I keep it on low on the neighbouring hob) and stir until this too is absorbed. Carry on in this vein, patiently, for another 10 minutes, then add the whole, just sautéed peas, and then start again, a ladleful of stock at a time. In about another 8 minutes or so the rice should be cooked and the risotto creamy. Taste to see if you need any more time or liquid. It's hard to be precise: sometimes you'll find you have stock left over; at others you'll need to add water from the kettle.

When you're happy with it, add the buttery pea and parmesan purée and beat it in well. Taste, season as needed, then beat in the remaining tablespoon of parmesan and any butter you may have left. You can sprinkle over some chopped flat-leaf parsley (and since I've got it growing in the garden I have no reason not to), but the lack of it won't give you any grief.

Serves 2.

Weekend Lunch

ALTHOUGH THE DINNER party remains the symbol of social eating, most eating in company among my friends actually takes place at weekend lunch. After a long day at work many of us are, frankly, too tired to go out and eat dinner, let alone cook it. And there is, as well, the baby factor. For many people of my generation, having to get food ready after the children have gone to bed explains the popularity of the Marks & Spencer menu. And even those who haven't got children are affected by the babysitting arrangements of their friends who have. When I was younger we stayed in bed at weekends until two in the afternoon: now that most of us are woken at six in the morning, there is a gap in the day where lunch can go. We have got into the habit of filling it.

Lunch is more forgiving than dinner: there isn't the dread engendered by perceived but not-quite-formulated expectations: there's no agenda, no aspirational model to follow, no socio-culinary challenge to which to rise; in short, no pressure. Lunch is just lunch.

And if you don't want to cook it, you don't have to. Saturday lunch can be at its most relaxed and pleasurable when it is just an indoor picnic. What matters, then, is what you buy. These days shopping is nobly recast as 'sourcing' – and clever you for finding the best chilli-marinaded olives, French sourdough bread or air-dried beef: certainly no shame for not clattering about with your own pots and pans instead.

Shopping is not necessarily the easy option. It's certainly not the cheap one. But discerning extravagance (rather than mere feckless vulgarity) can be immensely pleasurable. Indeed, I can find it positively uplifting: not for nothing is shopping known as retail therapy. Shopping for food is better than any other form of shopping. There's no trying-on for a start. Choosing the right cheese, the best and ripest tomato, the pinkest, sweetest ham can be intensely gratifying. And in shopping for food which you are then going to prepare (even if that preparation involves no more than de-bagging and unwrapping) there is also the glorious self-indulgence of knowing that you are giving pleasure to others.

Shopping is not a quick activity: you need to be prepared to proceed slowly, haltingly. Compromise can be ruinous. Of course, some of the time we all eat food that is less than perfect, less than enjoyable even, but you can't set out to buy inferior produce – what would be the point?

Good food doesn't have to be difficult to cook, and it

certainly doesn't need to be difficult to buy. But you must know what you're after. The important thing is to be greedy enough to get what's good, but not so restlessly greedy that you get too much of it. Restrict your choices, so that you provide lots of a few things rather than small amounts of many. This is partly an aesthetic dictate, partly a practical one. If you buy 100g slices of six different cheeses, everyone is going to feel inhibited about cutting some off; however generous you have been, it is only the meagreness of each portion that will be apparent. Provide, instead, a semblance – indeed the reality – of voluptuous abundance. You don't need to buy more than three different cheeses, but get great big fat wodges of each. You want munificence, you want plenty, you want people to feel they can eat as much as they want and there'll still be some left over afterwards. Start by thinking along the lines of one hard cheese, one soft cheese and maybe a blue cheese or chèvre. You needn't stick to this rigidly: sometimes it's good just to be seduced by the particular cheeses spread out in front of you on a cheese counter. Keep your head, though: without ruling out whim entirely, don't be immoderately ensnared by fanciful names or the provocatively unfamiliar. One type of cheese no one has heard of might well be interesting, but not three. Anyway, the desire to be interesting is possibly the most damaging impulse in cooking. Never worry about what your guests will think of you. Just think of the food. What will taste good?

And you don't have to go through the ridiculous

pantomime of pretending everything is homespun. If you're still getting your shopping out and unwrapping your packages when everyone arrives, who cares? Your kitchen doesn't have to look like a set from a 1950s American sitcom. It is curiously relaxing to be slowly creating the canvas – arranging the table, putting flowers in a vase, chopping up herbs and putting water on for potatoes – while talking and drinking unhurriedly with friends.

The shops nearest you will probably govern what sort of food you buy. I stick to the plainest basics: meat, cheese, bread; with tomatoes, a green salad, maybe some robustly salted, herb-speckled potatoes, the waxy fleshed, puce-skinned ones, cooked till sweet and soft then doused in oil, scarcely dribbled with vinegar or spritzed with lemon, and with a few feathery pieces of chopped zest on them, left to sit around to be eaten at room temperature.

If you're buying ham, get enough to cover a huge great plate with densely meaty pink slices. I sometimes buy both English ham, cut off the bone in the shop, and the cured Italian stuff. I like prosciutto di San Daniele better than prosciutto di Parma (the glorious, requisite, honeyed saltiness is more intense), but as long as it's well cut – and obviously freshly cut – so that each white-rimmed silky slice can be removed without sticking or tearing, that's fine: more than fine.

There is internal pressure in my home to buy bresaola, too, but although I like eating it well enough, I never mind if I don't. I'd rather buy a big, unpacketed, butcher-made pork pie, one which has a short, short flaky crust lined with clear salty jelly and then, within, densely packed smooth and peppery pork. Salame, too, is good. I don't think you need both salame and pie, so choose which you prefer. If you buy a whole little salame, as with the large pork pie, you can introduce an all-important DIY element into the proceedings: put it on a wooden board with a sharp knife and let people carve off for themselves thick, fat-pearled slices of spicy sausage. This way, the individual act of cutting, slicing, serving yourself, becomes almost a conversational tool. It makes people feel at home when they're around your kitchen table. Allow yourself a few saucer-sized plates of extras – maybe some fresh, marinated anchovies, olives steeped with shards of garlic and crumbled red chillies, astringent little cornichons, those ones that look like cartoon crocodiles in embryo, a soft, moussy slab of pâté – but, again, don't go overboard. I sometimes succumb to one of those Italian jars of olive-oil-soused blackened globes of chargrilled onions, sweet and smoky and wonderful with meat or cheese or a plain plate of bitter leaves.

If you prefer fish to meat, go for the old-fashioned traditional option: a huge plate of London-cure smoked salmon – mild, satiny and softly fleshy – with cornichons, lemon and maybe a pile of blinis, potato pancakes, a loaf or two of sandy soda bread, or thinly sliced and already buttered brown. If you have a delicatessen or fishmonger near you that sells a good enough version of the stuff, then maybe you should get a tentacled mess of Italianish seafood salad. I quite like, too, that old-fashioned pairing of tuna and beans. My Great-Aunt Myra, who was a wonderful cook, always used butter beans (just out of the tin, as was, of course, the olive-oil preserved tuna) and would gently mix the two, squeeze lemon over and cover with a fine net of wafer-thin onion rings. Yes, proper dried then soaked and cooked and drained real beans are always better, but there's something comforting and familiar for me in that quick and effort-free assembly. It tastes of my childhood.

Smoked salmon calls for brown bread, but there's something reassuring about a thick wedge of white bread, heavy with cold unsalted butter and curved over a tranche of quickly grabbed ham to make a casual sandwich. But all that matters is that the bread is good: sweet, sunflower-seed-studded brown, English bloomer or French bread – which could be a just-bought baguette or, my favourite, the slender ficelle. I sometimes think if I see another ciabatta I'll scream.

Frankly, if you can get good enough tomatoes, I'd just leave them as they are, whole, with a knife near by (a good, sharp, serrated one, suitable for the job) so that people can eat them in juicy red wedges with their bread and cheese, or cut them thinly and sprinkle with oil and salt to make their own private pools of tomato salad.

A green salad needn't comprise anything other than lettuce. All you need for dressing is good oil, a quick squeeze of lemon and a confident hand with the salt, tossed with your own bare hands. You can, of course, supplement the torn leaves (and let's be frank, most of us will be opening one of those cellophane packets) with some thin tongues of courgette (the slivers stripped off with the vegetable peeler), chopped spring onions or a handful of not-even-blanched sugar-snap peas or whatever you want. There's one proviso: keep it green. There is something depressingly institutional about cheerfully mixed salads. I was brought up like this: my mother was fanatical, and her aesthetic has seeped into my bloodstream; my father takes the same line. Do not even think of adding your tomatoes: keep them separate. Cucumber tends to make the salad weepy. Give it its own plate, and dress with peppery, mint-thick or dill-soused yoghurt or an old-fashioned sweet-sour vinaigrette.

In the same way, I am fanatical about keeping fruit separate. There is, for me, something so boarding-housey about the capacious bowl filled with waxy, dusty bananas, a few oranges, some pears and the odd shrunken apple. I want a plate of oranges, another of bananas, of apples, of pears. I even put black and white grapes on separate plates.

An unfussy lunch sprawled out on a Saturday definitely doesn't demand culinary high jinks. Don't worry about pudding. You just need some tubs of good ice-cream – there is a dangerously tempting large stock of them out there now – whichever make you like most. Or buy a tart from a good French pâtisserie.

Sunday lunch

PROPER SUNDAY LUNCH is everything contemporary cooking is not. Meat-heavy, hostile to innovation, resolutely formalised, it is as much ritual as meal, and an almost extinct ritual at that. Contemporary trends, it is true, have hastened a reappraisal of traditional cooking. But neither nostalgia for nursery foods nor an interest in ponderous culinary Victoriana is what Sunday lunch – Sunday dinner – is all about. It doesn't change, is impervious to considerations of health or fashion; it is about solidity, the family, the home.

One of the silent, inner promises I made myself on having children was to provide a home that made a reassuring, all-comers-welcome tradition of Sunday lunch. It hasn't materialised quite yet, but few of my generation lead meat-and-two-veg lives any more. We are generally more mobile, the weekend is no longer home-bound. Nor do we want to be kitchen-bound (and those with small children hardly have the time on their hands for involved cooking). The fact is that Sunday lunch is impossible to pull off without putting in at least a couple of hours by the sink and the stove. And it is far from being the sort of cooking anyway that finds favour now: the relaxed, let's throw this with that and come up with something simple and picturesquely rustic approach will not put a joint, Yorkshire pudding and roast potatoes on the table. To cook a decent Sunday lunch needs discipline and strict timekeeping.

But with modest organisation, there can be something strangely reassuring about cooking a traditional meal. It is about choreography, about timetabling, and has its own pleasures. We are so accustomed to being invited to consider cooking an art that we forget just how rewarding and satisfying it is as pure craft. My Latin teacher, Miss Plummer, who had the misfortune to teach at one of the less academic schools I frequented, used, with a sort of elegiac condescension, to remark that none of us could know the simple yet substantial pleasures of the carpenter in making a chair. But cooking does give that pleasure, and there are particular satisfactions peculiar to the making of Sunday lunch.

I love the solidity of it all: I don't mean by that the robust nature of the food alone, so much as the weighty texture of hospitality, of plain food warmly given. But it would be wrong to dwell too much on some notional and universally shared longing for a family group assembled around a big table, sharing food. There is that, maybe, but I think people tend to be frightened of cooking Sunday lunch themselves because of a fear or dread that is, frankly, family-induced. The still-remembered tensions of Sunday lunches of the past must be the underlying deterrent, rather than the cooking itself, in the present.

But it is possible to have a family lunch which dispenses, in any literal sense, with family (not that this is necessarily desirable). In the past, connections were familial; the boundaries were of blood. Today, people get their sense of extended family from their friends. I tend to find myself surrounded by people with small children. Others are differently bound.

Now, there is no reason on earth why you should feel it incumbent on yourself to get into a frenzy of batter-making and parsnip-peeling just because it is Sunday. And it's true that I might well have people over for Sunday lunch and give them pasta. The rule – if rule there can ever be – is the same rule that applies in any form of cooking: be honest; cook what you want to eat, not what you want to be seen eating.

Whenever I cook for people I find it easier to have scribbled down in front of me the times at which I'm meant to do any key thing – put things in the oven, take them out – just because once I start talking or drinking I tend to lose track. I haven't suggested this alongside any menus elsewhere because I can't know what time you'll be eating and anyway have tried not to be too bossy. With full-on Sunday lunch, I have no such compunction. It has to be planned as efficiently as a military campaign.

Traditional Sunday lunch does, of course, mean beef. As for cuts: it helps here as well to go to a butcher rather than the supermarket. You can explain what you want, or ask what you think you should want, for how many people, how you want to carve it and so on. Rib of beef gives the best flavour, but it is very difficult to carve. I am a hopeless carver and believe that in cooking especially, though in everything really, it is better to play to your strengths than your weaknesses. Besides, if you can't do much more than hack at it, it's a waste. I am resigned to buying a boned joint. I have recently become very extravagant and gone for contrefilet; a boned sirloin would be good, too, though.

I have always found gravy problematic, but for beef I don't think you can casually deglaze the roasting dish with some red wine and hope it'll be all right. Nor does that mean the opposite extreme: the thick, floury, school gloop. Banish instant gravy powders and granules from your thoughts and your store cupboards. Instead, start caramelising your onions early, and cook them slowly. This may be difficult when you're trying to orchestrate everything else for lunch, but you can easily do the gravy the day before and then just reheat and add meat juices at the last minute.

Roast potatoes are another fraught area. I have, in the past, got frantic with despair as the time for the meat to be ready drew closer and the potatoes were still blond and untroubled in their roasting pan. The key here is to get the fat hotter than you would believe necessary before you start and to continue to cook the potatoes at a higher heat and for longer than you might believe possible. And you must roughen them up after parboiling.

The heat of the fat is again the crucial element in making a Yorkshire pudding rise. There's no doubt this is easier if you have two ovens (one for the beef, one for the Yorkshire pudding), but the beef can either be cooked at a very high temperature for a quick blast and then at a moderate one for a while or at a highish one all the time. You can always blast the Yorkshire pudding on a high heat while the beef is resting on its carving board.

Roast root vegetables are traditional, but I tend not to bother. With the roast potatoes and Yorkshire pudding, you hardly need more starch, though if I'm cooking roast pork, or roast beef without the Yorkshire pudding, or the usual roast chicken, I might do parsnips, either roasted alongside the potatoes, or anointed with honey in another pan and put in the oven to grow sweet and burnished.

As for other vegetables, I think you need two sorts. This can make life difficult, but not insurmountably so. It's just a matter, again, of time management: the important thing is not suddenly to need about 6 pans on a 4-hob stove. And there doesn't need to be too much chopping. Choose, for example, frozen peas and something to provide fresh, green crunch: beans, Savoy cabbage, pak choi. I love broccoli, but it is very sweet, and with the peas you don't really need any more sweetness. It's unconventional, but I do rather like a tomato salad somewhere too, especially if it's still warm outside.

I don't often make my own horseradish sauce – I buy a good bottled one and add a bit of crème fraîche, ordinary cream or Greek yoghurt – but mustard must, for me, be English and made up at the last minute. I don't mind having other mustards on the table but, for me, the whole meal is ruined without proper English mustard.

Traditionalists will insist on a sturdy pie or crumble for pudding, but really, after all that carbohydrate, have you got room? I am immensely greedy, but I don't like that invasive and uncomfortable feeling of bloatedness that can make you regret eating much more than a hangover can ever make you regret drinking.

Now that you seem to be able to get blueberries all the year round, I often serve them with a large, shallow bowl of Barbados cream. This – yoghurt and double cream stirred together, fudgy brown sugar sprinkled on top – has the advantage of having to be done the day before. I love lemon ice-cream after this (and it's good with blueberries, or indeed any berries, too) and I sometimes make one that doesn't need fiddling about with while freezing – you just bung it in the freezer. Nothing is quite as good as proper ice-cream, made with a custard base and then churned until solid, but home cooking is based on compromises, and a simple pudding is a compromise I am often grateful to make. You could consider a crumble if only because the crumble mixture can be made up earlier and just sprinkled on the fruit as you sit down and cooked while you eat the beef. Remember: you are not trying to produce the definitive Sunday lunch to end all Sunday lunches. Nor are you a performance artist. The idea is to make a lunch which you want to eat and can imagine sitting down to do so without bursting into tears.

I'M SORRY TO sound bossy, but Sunday lunch, as I've said, has to be run like a military campaign. I find it easier to decide when I want to eat and then work backwards, writing every move down on a pad which I keep in a fixed place in the kitchen. This timetable is engineered towards having lunch ready to eat at 2pm exactly. I take it for granted that pudding's been made already.

All quantities and timings have in mind a lunch for about 6 adults and perhaps some children and are based on having a 2¼kg joint to cook.

11.20	Start gravy
11.30	Take beef out of fridge
11.50	Peel potatoes
12.05	Put the potatoes in their water in the pan, bring to the boil and parboil. Preheat oven to gas mark 7/210°C
12.15	Put roasting pan in oven with a knob of dripping for beef
12.20	Put beef in
12.35	Prepare any veg that need chopping or cleaning, etc.
12.40	Put pan with dripping for potatoes in oven
12.50	Make Yorkshire pudding
1.00	Put potatoes in
1.05	Prepare veg. Turn on plate warmer or hot cupboard
1.25	Put veg water on
1.35	Put pan with dripping for Yorkshire pudding in oven
1.40	Take out beef and put in Yorkshire pudding, turning oven up to gas mark 8/220°C as you do so. Let beef stand
1.45	Cook vegetables
2.00	Take out Yorkshire pudding and potatoes

The roast beef

I think many people underplay how much meat you need. For 6 people, I wouldn't consider getting under 2¼kg (or

5lb), which, in other words, is about 375g per person. A joint is a sad prospect without the possibility of leftovers. For a rib you should add on about 1kg extra here.

For rare meat you can either cook the beef at the highest possible temperature for 15 minutes and then turn it down to gas mark 4/180°C and cook for 15 minutes per lb (I still find it easier to calculate the cooking time per lb) or at gas mark 7/210°C throughout for 15 minutes per lb, which is what I did here. Think of 15 minutes per lb as about 33 minutes per kg. I usually do 15 minutes per lb and then add on an extra 5 minutes so that those who don't like rare meat have a bit of slightly more cooked beef from the ends. Those who don't like blood don't have to get it: the rest of us gratifyingly do.

All I do to the beef is to massage it with dry mustard powder after I've taken it out of the fridge. I use a knob of dripping for the pan, but you could use whatever fat you have to hand.

The gravy

Gravy is one of my weaknesses, which is to say I find it hard to make a convincing light and thin juice. To overcome my deficiencies I took to following Jane Grigson's recipe for onion gravy (indeed most of my Sunday is Grigson-based), adding a drop of Marsala to it. You don't need to – you could use some Madeira or even some sweet sherry or just add a little bit more sugar – but the Marsala brings a wonderful aromatic muskiness to the gravy. If I don't have any real beef stock, I use a tub of good fresh beef stock. You can use a stock cube (try an Italian one), in which case use it well diluted and taste before putting in any more salt.

You can start the gravy the day before if you want, just reheating and adding meat juices at the last minute.

15g butter, and a dribble of oil or dripping
1 onion, sliced very thinly in the food processor
pinch brown sugar
2 tablespoons Marsala
1 teaspoon flour
300ml beef stock

Melt the butter (with the oil or dripping to stop it burning) in a saucepan and cook the onion in it at a very low temperature, stirring often. When the onion is soft add the sugar and Marsala and let it caramelise. Cover with foil, putting the foil as near to the bottom of the pan as possible and continue to cook, still on a very low flame, for about 10 minutes. Then stir in the flour and cook, stirring, for about 2 minutes. Stir in the stock, bring to the boil (you can turn the heat up here) then reduce the heat to very low again and simmer gently for about 20 minutes. Purée in the food processor (or you can strain it, pushing the soft onion through the sieve). Pour back into the saucepan. At the last minute, reheat and add meat juices from roasting pan. This gravy is wonderfully stress-free, since you don't have to be doing furious deglazing at the last minute.

The roast potatoes

I like roast potatoes fairly small, so I cut a medium-to-large one into about 3. For 6 people, I suppose, that's about

1¾kg. Well, that may be over-generous, but nothing is worse than too few.

Peel the potatoes and cut them into large chunks. Put them in cold salted water, bring to the boil and parboil for 4–5 minutes. Drain, put back in the saucepan, put on the lid and bang the whole thing about a bit so that the edges of the potatoes get blurred: the rough edges help them catch in the fat and so get crisp. Add 1 tablespoon or so of semolina and give the pan, with its lid on, another good shake. The semolina gives the potatoes a divinely sweet edge: not at all cloying or inappropriate, just an intensified caughtness, as it were. When my mother and aunts were young, they had an Italian au pair, Antonia, who, when required to make a British Sunday lunch (having never cooked anything other than Italian food), adopted, or rather invented, this practice. If you're unconvinced, or don't have any semolina to hand, just use flour and shake the warm potatoes around in it. The flour doesn't give the same honey-toned depth as semolina, but helps the potatoes catch and brown wonderfully.

It's essential that the fat's hot before the potatoes go in. I use 2 tablespoon-sized lumps of goose fat or some truly superb grass-fed beef dripping. If you can lay your hands on neither, of course you can use oil or even vegetable fat. The potatoes must not be taken out of the oven until you are absolutely ready to eat them. They will take approximately an hour to cook.

The Yorkshire pudding

I always use Jane Grigson's *English Food* for the Chinese Yorkshire pudding recipe, which is not as odd as it sounds. The story is that when a big competition was held in Leeds for the best Yorkshire pudding, the winner was a Chinese cook called Tin Sung Yang. For years it was held to have a mystery ingredient – tai luk sauce – until, Jane Grigson reports, a niece of hers found that this was a Chinese joke. Nevertheless, the recipe is different from normal: it works backwards. That's to say, you mix the eggs and milk and then stir in the flour, rather than making a well in the flour and adding the eggs and milk: and it works triumphantly; it billows up into a gloriously copper crown of a cushion. I am able to cook this for the most die-hard, pudding-proud northerners without inhibition or anxiety. I prefer Yorkshire pudding to be in one dish rather than in those depressing, canteen-style individual portions, so for this amount, I use an enamel dish about 30cm by 19cm and 7cm deep. Cook it on the top shelf of the oven but make sure the shelf isn't too high up as the Yorkshire pudding really does rise. I have had to prise it off the ceiling of the oven, which slightly dented its magnificence and my glory.

300ml milk
4 eggs
250g plain flour, sifted

Mix all the ingredients, except the flour, with pepper and a scant ½ teaspoon of salt, beating them well together. I use my free-standing mixer, the fabulous American KitchenAid, but anything – hand-held electric mixer, rotary or balloon whisk – would do. Let these ingredients stand for 15 minutes and then whisk in the flour. Meanwhile put the pan with 1 tablespoon or so of dripping or whatever other fat you're using in a very high oven. Into this intensely hot pan you should pour the batter, when you're ready for it, and cook for 20 minutes. Bring it, triumphant, to the table.

Calming winter lunch for 6

Roast pork loin with roast leeks

Clapshot with burnt onions

Custard tart

MUCH AS I LOVE proper roast leg of pork with its carapace of amber-glazed crackling, I don't cook it that much: roast boned and rolled loin is my more regular pig-out. I feel at ease with it, even though the flesh can tend to dry stringiness. Ask the butcher for rib-end of loin (hard to carve, but wonderful tasting). And put a little liquid in the roasting pan so the meat grows tender in its own small pool of odoriferous steam. Anything will do: a glass of wine or cider, some stock, water mixed with apple juice, the leftover liquid you've cooked carrots in.

Cooking boned and rolled pork loin bears almost any interpretation or elaboration. By elaboration, I mean not to imply complexity of culinary arrangement but wide-rangingness. If you want, at other times, to add a modern, fusiony note, make a paste of garlic and root ginger and smear that over, rubbing ground ginger into the prepared and removed rind for hot crackling; if you want something altogether less vibrant, then pulverise some dried bay leaves, and press these against the soft covering of white fat. Or rub in ground cloves, cinnamon and cardamom to produce an almost – if inappropriate – Middle Eastern waft. Neither of these requires crackling; here you would be after altogether less strenuous eating.

Get the butcher to remove the bones and give them to you, so you can cook them around the joint, which will make the gravy. And while you're about it, ask him to chop them up small. As for the rind: if you want crackling, ask him to remove the rind, score it and give it back to you; and, even if you don't want crackling, the loin should be left elegantly wrapped in its pearly coating of fat. If there's not enough fat on the joint, it will end up too dry.

Roast loin of pork

You will need about 1.8kg boned, derinded weight, which means a joint, before butchering, in the region of 2½kg. If you're a good carver, don't bother with boning. Either way, the crackling should be cooked separately.

Preheat the oven to gas mark 7/210°C. Work out how long the loin needs – and at roughly 45 minutes per kg, for a 1.8kg joint that's about 70 minutes – and cook the loin in its pan on one shelf, and, putting it in about 45 minutes before you want to eat, the crackling on a rack over a roasting tray on another shelf. About halfway through the pork's cooking time throw a glass of wine (or whatever you're using; cider would be very good here) into the pan.

Some people simply get the rind removed and then drape it over the loin as it cooks. The reason I don't do this is because then you have to do a real number to rid the juices in the meat dish of fat. I am not one of nature's gravy makers, and therefore I do everything to make life easier for myself – and frankly suggest you do too. As for this gravy: all you need to do – having cooked the crackling in a separate pan – is pour the winey juices from the meat dish into a sauceboat or bowl, removing fat if you can and if you need to. Taste it: you may need to add a little bit of water, you may just want to use it as is. I am not on the whole a thick-gravy person: you may be.

Roast leeks

For 6 people, get about 8 not too fat leeks (although one each would probably be enough, I'd always rather have over). Once you've made sure they're clean, cut them on the diagonal into logs about 8cm long. Pour some olive oil in a roasting tray and turn the leeks in them so they're glossy all over. Sprinkle over some coarse sea salt and roast for about 30 minutes at gas mark 7/210°C, I usually roast them at a higher temperature and for slightly less time, but it would be absurd to complicate matters since you're going to have the oven at mark 7 anyway.

I love these leeks blistered sweet on the outside, suggestively oniony within their slithery centre. I know that there are going to be onions themselves with the clapshot, but the pork can take the double helping of allium. If you feel otherwise, make a large, iron-dark bowl of butter-drenched kale. Kale, indeed, is a feature of traditional clapshot; this recipe makes do without and it is tempting to make up the shortfall. If you wanted to add a slightly more modern touch, then simply get some pak choi or choi sum (which most supermarkets seem to stock now) and steam or stir-fry it with or without lacily grated ginger.

Clapshot with burnt onions

I got the idea for this in the *Tesco Recipe Collection* of October 1996 in an article written by Catherine Brown. It is a modern take on a traditional dish, which was a hodgepodge of various vegetables cooked and mushed together. This is something not so stylish as to be self-conscious, but not so hearty as to be indigestible.

1kg swede, peeled and diced
1kg floury potatoes, such as golden wonder, King Edward or Kerr's Pink, peeled and quartered
100g butter
fresh nutmeg

for the burnt onions
4 tablespoons olive oil
2 large strong onions, very thinly sliced
2 tablespoons caster sugar

First, make the clapshot: put the swede in a pan of boiling, salted water, and simmer for about 5 minutes. Add the potatoes and simmer for about 25–30 more minutes until both are just cooked. Don't overcook or they will disintegrate into potato soup. Drain thoroughly.

Dry the swede and potato slightly by putting them back in the saucepan (which you've wiped dry) and placing it over a low heat. Then mash – with a potato ricer or mouli – with the butter. Season to taste, adding a good grating of fresh nutmeg.

While the potatoes and swede are cooking, get started with the onion-burning. Heat the oil in a heavy-based frying pan over low heat. Slice the onions very finely (I use the processor for this), add to the oil and cook slowly for about 30 minutes until crisp and golden brown, stirring and scraping from time to time. Turn heat to high and sprinkle with sugar and stir continuously for a further 3 minutes or so until the sugar caramelises and the onion darkens.

Put the clapshot in a serving bowl and top with the burnt onions.

Custard tart

I adore custard tart: I love its barely-vanilla-scented, nutmeggy softness, the silky texture of that buttermilk-coloured eggy cream, solidified just enough to be carved into trembling wedges on the plate. It isn't hard to make, but I botch it often out of sheer clumsiness. But now I have learnt my lessons, and pass them on to you. One: pour the custard into the pastry case while the pastry case is in the oven, so that you don't end up leaving a trail from kitchen counter to cooker, soaking the pastry case in the process. And two: don't be so keen to use up every last scrap of that custard, filling the case right to the very brim so that it's bound – as you knew it was – to spill, making it soggy and ruining the contrast between crisp crust and tender filling. If you can manage not to do both those things, then you can make a perfect custard pie. I won't promise it's an easy exercise, though.

If you want to eat it cold, this makes life easier as you can arrange to have free play with the oven the day before. But, at its best, the custard should still have a memory of heat about it. Make it before you put the pork in the oven and let it sit for 1½ hours or thereabouts, gently subsiding into muted warmth in the kitchen.

If you can't be bothered to make the pastry yourself you have a choice: either you can use bought shortcrust or don't bother with a crust at all and make a baked custard. For a baked custard, make double quantities of custard, then pour it into a pie dish (with a capacity of just over 1 litre), stand the pie dish in a roasting tin filled with hot water and bake in a gas mark 2/150°C oven for about 1 hour.

If you don't keep vanilla sugar – although I do recommend it, see page 52 – then just add a few drops of real vanilla extract to the mixture. Of course you can always add an actual vanilla pod to the milk and cream when you warm them, but actually I don't like baked custard with too much vanilla: I like the merest musky suggestion of it.

for the pastry

120g plain flour, preferably Italian 00
30g icing sugar
80g cold butter
1 egg yolk
1/2 teaspoon pure vanilla extract
1 egg white (leftover from yolk for custard) to seal

for the custard

3 eggs	**150ml milk**
1 egg yolk	**pinch ground mace**
2 tablespoons vanilla sugar	**freshly grated nutmeg**
300ml single cream	

To make the pastry sift the flour and icing sugar into a dish and add the cold butter, cut into small cubes. Put this dish, just as it is, in the deep-freeze for 10 minutes. In a small bowl beat the egg yolk with the vanilla extract, a tablespoon of iced water and a pinch of salt. Put this bowl in the fridge. When the 10 minutes are up, put the flour and butter in a processor with the double blade fitted or in a mixer with the flat paddle on slow and turn on. After barely a minute, the mixture will begin to resemble oatmeal or flattened breadcrumbs, and this is when you add the yolk mixture. Be prepared to add more iced water, drop by cautious drop, until you have a nearly coherent dough. Then scoop it out, still just crumbly, push it into a fat disc, cover with clingfilm and stick in the fridge for 20 minutes. Preheat the oven to gas mark 6/200°C.

Roll out the pastry fairly thinly. Line a deep flan or quiche case with the pastry and bake blind for about 20 minutes. Take out of the oven and remove the beans and paper or foil. Beat the egg white lightly, brush the bottom and sides of the cooked pastry case with it (the idea being to seal the pastry so the custard won't make it soggy later on) and put back in the oven for 5 minutes. Turn down the oven to gas mark 3/160°C.

Put the eggs, egg yolks and sugar in a bowl and whisk together. Warm the cream and milk in a saucepan with the mace and pour into the egg and sugar mixture. Stir to mix and then strain into the pastry case, as it sits in the pulled-out rack in the oven. Grate over some nutmeg. Push the shelf back in carefully but confidently (tense hesitation can be disastrous: far too jerky), shut the door and leave the custard pie in the oven to bake for about 45 minutes. Take a look though, after about 35 minutes. The custard, when it's ready, should look more or less solid but still with a tremble at its centre.

Take out of the oven, grate some more nutmeg over and leave until it reaches tepid heaven.

Dinner

I'M NOT SURE I like the connotations of the term Dinner Party, but I think we're stuck with it. Kitchen Suppers – which is perhaps what this chapter should be called – sounds altogether too twee, even if it evokes more accurately the culinary environment most of us now inhabit. So let's just call it dinner, which is what it is. The modern dinner party was the invention of the post-war, post-Elizabeth David brigade of socially aware operators: this was the age of Entertaining-with-a-capital-E. Not only was the food distinctly not home food, it wasn't even restaurant food: what was evoked was the great ambassadorial dinner. But *autres temps, autres moeurs*: most of us don't even have dining-rooms any more. Yet people still think they should be following the old culinary agenda: they feel it is incumbent on them not so much to cook as to slave, to strive, to sweat, to *perform*. Life doesn't have to be like that. As far as I'm concerned, moreover, it shouldn't be like that. I find formality constraining. I don't like fancy, arranged napkins and I don't like fancy, arranged food.

That's not to say that I feel everything should be artfully casual: the this-is-just-something-I've-thrown-together school of cookery can be just as pretentious. What I feel passionately is that home food is home food, even when you invite other people to eat it with you. It shouldn't be laboriously executed, daintily arranged, individually portioned. It's relaxed, expansive, authentic: it should reflect your personality not your aspirations. Professional chefs have to innovate, to elaborate, to impress the paying customer. But the home cook is under no such constraints. (Indeed, you don't have to cook much at all if you are prepared to shop well.) I once went to a dinner party a good friend of mine gave, and she was so anxious, she'd been up till three in the morning the night before making stocks. She said scarcely a word to any of us after opening the door, since she was in the middle of the first of about five courses. The food was spectacular: but she spent most of the evening ever-more hysterical in the kitchen. At one point we could, as we stiltedly made conversation between ourselves, hear her crying. The fault wasn't her competence, but her conception: she felt that her dinner party must be a showcase for her culinary talents and that we must all be judging her. Some cooks, indeed, seem to resent their guests for interrupting the cooking, rather as doctors and nurses resent patients for interrupting the nice, efficient running of their hospitals.

Restaurants need to be able to produce food in short order. But unless you want to stand in your kitchen handing hot plates out to your friends at the table, you need not and should not. Avoid small portions of tender-fleshed fish that have to be conjured up at the last minute and *à point*, and anything that will wilt, grow soggy or lose character or hope as it sits, sideboard-bound and dished up. Don't make life harder on yourself. I am working on banishing the starter from my dinner-partying life. (Truth to tell, I don't have much of a dinner-partying life: but, in theory, I do invite friends for dinner.) This is not so much because cooking the starter is difficult – in fact it is the easiest course of any of them – but because clearing the table, timetabling the whole meal, keeping the main course warm, can all add to the general tension of the evening.

Besides, our lives are so different now. Because working hours are longer, we eat dinner later. And if dinner doesn't start till nine or nine-thirty, then it is going to be a very late evening if you sit down to three courses. And you don't want to miss out on the general hanging around with a drink beforehand. I am more of an eater than a drinker and tend to get unbearably anxious if the drinking goes on for hours with no sign of the eating to come, so I try to amalgamate the two. I am, in effect, not really banishing the starter, but relocating it, refashioning it. Now, I can't pretend that serving bits with drinks is an original idea, but I suggest that you think of them as the starter. There is no dinner party I would give where I couldn't just make a plate of crostini to eat as a first course.

Normally, I make a couple of different sorts. I don't assemble the crostini in advance, but I often make the mixture with which they're going to be spread days ahead and keep slices for toast, ready-carved from baguette or ficelle, bagged up in the freezer.

Indian-summer dinner for 6

Pea and lettuce soup

Lamb with chick peas

Couscous salad

Turkish delight figs with pistachio crescents

THIS IS THE SORT of food to eat when the days are unexpectedly warm, but the nights are nevertheless beginning to get cooler. You're still in the mood for summer food, but you need ballast too. This food is as suited for eating on a table in the garden as it is for a windows-shut, curtains-closed dinner inside.

Pea and lettuce soup

Shell the fresh peas. Then make a stock with the pods, some parsley stalks, peppercorns, onion, half a carrot and a stick of celery and, of course, water. If I don't feel like tackling fresh peas, or they're not available, I use frozen petits pois and either chicken stock or vegetable stock powder. I find it easier to start the soup off with thawed peas, but if they're still frozen it couldn't matter less. If you've got any basil-infused oil you can use that for softening the vegetables at the beginning. I know mint is the usual herb here, but basil seems to enhance the fruity sweetness of the peas.

2 tablespoons olive oil
4 spring onions, sliced finely
zest of ½ lemon
1 ½ kg fresh peas, podded or 500g packet frozen petits pois
1 English round lettuce, roughly chopped
1 ¼ litres light stock (see above)
1 teaspoon sugar
1 tablespoon dry sherry
3–4 tablespoons double cream
small plant or large handful basil

Put the oil in the pan and when it's warm add the very finely sliced spring onions and lemon zest, stir a bit and then add the peas. Turn well in the oil and then add the lettuce and cook till it wilts and then collapses into the peas. Pour over the stock, sprinkle over the sugar and bring to the boil. Turn down to a simmer and cook gently and uncovered till the peas are soft, about 10 minutes. Purée in batches, in a blender if possible. You don't get that velvety emulsion with a processor, though you can sieve it after processing, which will do it. Or just use the mouli.

Pour back into the saucepan, add the sherry and cook for a minute or so before tasting to see what else the soup needs, bearing in mind you'll be adding some cream and eating it cold. Let it cool a little, then stir in the cream and let it cool properly before putting it in a tureen and into the fridge.

Just as you're about to eat, taste for more salt or pepper, add more cream if wanted, and then shred the basil and add a good bit to each bowlful after ladling it out from the tureen.

Lamb with chick peas

It's up to you whether you use whole noisette rolls, which you roast and then slice, or individual noisette discs, which you grill, griddle or fry; the former taste better, but the latter look better. I can never carve from the entire rolled joint without it unfurling all over the place, but of course you do get the tender, uncharred sides from the middle of the roll. When you cook the individual noisettes, you're sealing each slice in the heat. But the marinade will help to make it tender. Make sure that you're using the best lamb you can afford.

If you're going for the whole-roll option, think along the lines of getting 3 x 400g noisettes (although I might well get 4), and then roast them in a gas mark 7/210°C oven for 20–40 minutes, depending on your oven and the age and thickness of the meat.

As for the individual noisettes, I work on the assumption that you have to give each person 2, and then allow for half of those present to have more.

I think it's easier to cook the chick peas in advance and do the lamb on the evening itself, having put it in its marinade the night before or the morning of your dinner.

Soak 500g chick peas in abundant water, and with a paste made from 3 tablespoons flour, 3 tablespoons salt and 1 tablespoon bicarbonate of soda (as on page 62). Leave for 24 hours. Drain, running the cold tap over them in the colander as you do so, then put them in a pan with 5 cloves of garlic, peeled and bashed, 2 bay leaves, 2 small onions, peeled but left whole (makes them easier to remove later) and the needles from a large sprig of rosemary. The bitter, boiled shards of rosemary will get in everyone's teeth, and ruin the creamy sweetness of the cooked chick peas, so put them in a bag or tea infuser.

Cover again with abundant water, add 1 tablespoon olive oil, put the lid on and bring to the boil, but do not open the pan; you'll have to listen closely to hear when it's starting to boil. Turn down slightly, and let the chick peas cook at a simmer for about 2 hours. You can check them after 1½ hours, but keep the lid on till then. When tender, drain, reserving a mugful of the cooking liquid. Leave, even up to a couple of days, till you want to eat. It would be better to remove the skins around each butterscotch-coloured pea, and I often start doing this, but have never yet completed the task.

To reheat, put 8 tablespoons olive oil and 6 cloves garlic, peeled and chopped, in a large, wide pan on moderate heat. I like to use a terracotta pot for this. Add to this 1–2 fresh red chillies, seeded and finely chopped, or crumble in a dried chilli pepper. Add the drained chick peas and turn well. Meanwhile, take 3 good-sized tomatoes, blanched, peeled, deseeded, roughly chopped and add to the chick peas. Salt very generously, stir well and taste; you may need to add some of the cooking liquid. You don't want this mushy exactly, but you want a degree of fusion, of fuzziness around the edges. Take off the heat, and cover until you've dealt with the lamb.

FOR 15 NOISETTES of lamb, make a marinade out of 10 tablespoons olive oil, 4 cloves garlic, crushed, 1 red onion, peeled and chopped, and 1 small fresh red chilli pepper, seeded and sliced. I find the easiest, most efficient way of doing this is by dividing everything between 2 plastic bags. Leave overnight or for as long as you can.

Just before you're about to sit down for your first course, take the lamb out of its marinade. You can drain the marinade and use that in place of the olive oil for sauté-ing the chick peas, above; in which case use a smaller amount of chilli. Cook the lamb either by frying in a cast-iron pan on a griddle, or giving it a few minutes each side under a very hot grill, or sear the meat in a pan then give them about 10 minutes in a gas mark 7/210°C oven. To keep the lamb pieces warm, leave them in a low oven on a dish covered with foil while you eat your soup.

When you serve, arrange the chick peas on a big, flattish bowl (again a terracotta one is perfect) or a couple of big plates and place the lamb over them. Chop over some fresh, flat-leaf parsley, or coriander if you feel infused with the mood of late-summer headiness.

Couscous salad

Sometimes I provide just a couple of small bowls filled with well-chopped red onion for people to sprinkle over the lamb and chick peas as they like. The alternative is a couscous salad, which in effect is panzanella, only using couscous in place of the bread. I often put basil in it, but this dinner has enough going on as it is without introducing another forceful character, so I suggest parsley.

200g couscous
6 tablespoons olive oil
2–3 tablespoons best red wine vinegar
6 good tomatoes
½–1 small red onion, to taste
1 cucumber
1 bunch parsley, to yield approx. 8 tablespoons chopped

Put the couscous into a bowl with 1 teaspoon salt and pour over 250ml boiling water. Cover and leave for 15 minutes. Fluff up with a fork and add the olive oil, 2 tablespoons of the vinegar and some pepper and put in another bowl (or leave in the same one if you're in no hurry) to cool. Prepare the tomatoes by blanching, peeling, deseeding and dicing, only make sure you don't leave them in the hot water too long. Cut the flesh into neat small dice. Chop the red onion up small. You can leave these, separately, until you want to eat. The rest I'd do at the last minute.

That's to say, when you're about to put the main course on the table, dice the cucumber and stir, along with the tomatoes, onion and 7 tablespoons of parsley, into the couscous with a fork. Add salt and more vinegar if you think it needs it.

Arrange on a plate and sprinkle on the remaining parsley.

Turkish delight figs

With thanks to Pat Harrison and Masterchef

How to say this without sounding ungracious? But I would never have expected to find such an easy, straightforward recipe on *Masterchef*. They're beautiful but not in an art-directed way: the purple-blue figs are cut to reveal the gaping red within, so that they sit in their bowl like plump little open-mouthed birds. When they're slicked with the flower-scented syrup, they become imbued with Middle Eastern sugariness, and the aromatic liquid itself absorbs and takes on a glassy pink from the figs. Perfect symbiosis.

Two figs a head should do it – they are very sweet, very intense – but if you can find only small figs, increase this to 3 per person. They're wonderful, anyway, the next day.

175g sugar
30ml/2 tablespoons rosewater
30ml/2 tablespoons orange-flower water
juice of 1 lemon
12 ripe, black figs

Dissolve the sugar in 175ml water in a small, heavy-based saucepan over a low heat. Increase the heat, bring to the boil and boil rapidly for 5 minutes. Add the rosewater, orange-flower water and lemon juice. Bring back to the boil and simmer for 2 minutes.

Carefully cut the figs vertically into quarters, leaving them intact at the base. Arrange on a flat, heatproof dish and spoon the hot syrup over them. Set aside to cool, basting with the syrup occasionally. Serve at room temperature, with Greek yoghurt and pistachio crescent biscuits (below).

The accompanying biscuits with the original recipe were sesame seed and cinnamon scented. I make instead these pistachio crescents, rich and tender, almost soft and definitely friable. But not hard to do. And the aromatic grittiness and moon-curled shapes give a one-thousand-and-one-nights feel, which is just right with the rosewater scent of the fig-basting syrup.

Pistachio crescents

These are rather like the hazelnut-smoky Middle-European Kipferln sold in expensive late-night supermarkets: densely powdery within, compounded by the blanket of icing sugar with which they are thickly, mufflingly covered. The amount below will make 12 biscuits.

75g pistachios (shelled weight)
60g soft unsalted butter
15g icing sugar, sifted
45g plain flour, preferably Italian 00, sifted
pinch salt

Preheat the oven to gas mark 3/160°C. Grease 2–3 baking sheets or, better still, cover them with Bake-o-Glide.

Toast the pistachios by frying them in a thick-bottomed frying pan with no fat for a few minutes so that their rich, waxy aroma is released. Pour into the bowl of the food processor and blitz until pulverised. You can buy ground pistachios from Middle Eastern shops – and I often do – but the varied, both nubbly and dusty, texture of the home-pulverised ones is good here.

With a wooden spoon, beat the butter until creamy – you are getting it ready to absorb the sugar with hardly any additional beating – and then duly add the icing sugar. I just spoon it into a tea strainer suspended over the bowl with the butter and push it through. Beat a while longer, until butter and sugar are light and incorporated, almost liquid-soft, and then add the sifted flour and salt. Keep stirring composedly and then add the ground pistachios, beating until just mixed. The dough will be sticky but firm enough to mould with your hands. If it feels too mushy, put it in the fridge for 10–20 minutes. To make the half-moons, flour your hands lightly and then take out small lumps of the dough – about 1 scant tablespoon at a time if you were measuring it, but I don't suggest you do: this is for guidance only – and roll them between your hands into sausages about 6cm long. Slightly flatten the sausage as you curl it round to form a little bulging snake of a crescent and put on the prepared baking sheet. Carry on until all the dough mixture is used up. And, by the way, don't be alarmed at how green these snakes look: cooked and dredged with icing sugar the intense lichen-coloured glow will fade.

Bake in the preheated oven for about 25 minutes, though start checking after 15. The softness should be just below the surface: take them out when the tops are firm and beginning to go blondly brown. Let the crescents sit on their baking sheets out of the oven for a few minutes and then remove to a wire rack. Go carefully: they are, as I said earlier, intensely friable. Dredge them with icing sugar very thickly indeed (again, I use a teaspoon to push the powder through a tea strainer) and leave to cool. You can do these ahead, and just dust over a little more icing sugar as you serve them.

Afterword

WHAT I'VE DISCOVERED, after what feels like a lifetime's cooking, is that anything which holds true in the kitchen, is just as true out of the kitchen. This is one of my mantras and I fear it won't be the last time you hear me chant it. And I'm sorry if it reeks of homespun philosophy, but that's just what it is. So, while it may be the case that occasionally – at the end of a long day or when I'm so exhausted that just staying upright seems a challenge – I approach cooking with something less than my usual gusto, I nearly always find that just getting on with it can make me wonder what I was dreading in the first place, and why. But then, the same applies to so many obligations and undertakings that loom over us in life, outside of the kitchen, too. Fear – of disappointment, inadequacy, failure – seems to make fools of us, causing us to forget what we all unfailingly learn from experience: that not doing what frightens us makes us fear it more rather than less. Perhaps some day I'll write a book called 'Feel the Fear and Cook it Anyway', although to some extent I suspect that this is, indeed, the subliminal message of every book I've ever written.

I understand why cooking can hold so much terror and the kitchen seem a place of stress not solace. I'm sure this is partly to do with the contemporary cult of the chef, and is further fuelled by the hysterical pursuit of perfection that defines the age we live in. I am not a chef, am horrified when thus defined and resist, without a shred of disingenuousness, the miscast role of expert. Again and again, I say and can never seem to say enough: if we really needed qualifications and expertise before we stepped into the kitchen, human beings would have fallen out of the evolutionary loop a long time ago.

I don't believe that cooking holds any inherent moral qualities or reveals essential purity of purpose and congratulation-worthy virtue. Certainly not: it wouldn't occur to me to feel guilty about eating food I hadn't cooked – so long as I enjoyed it – any more than I ever have or would feel guilty about buying clothes rather than sewing something to wear myself. The born-again fervour and judgemental outlook of the status-conscious cook seem to me positively to preclude a happy life in the kitchen – or, indeed, out of it. I don't cook because I feel I ought to, but because I want to. And, of course, there are times when I don't want to. That's life. Sometimes reality has the edge over romance: albeit I have said before, and hand-on-heart declare again, that for me the kitchen is not a place I want to escape from, but to escape *to*.

The kitchen is not a place I want to escape from but to escape to

© MasterChef Australia

NIGELLA LAWSON IS one of the world's best-loved food writers. She learned to cook in her mother's kitchen as a child, balancing on a rickety stool pushed up against the stove.

Nigella was Deputy Literary Editor of the *Sunday Times* and wrote a food column for *Vogue* before becoming a food writer full-time.

Her first book *How to Eat* (on which this book was based) was published in 1998, bringing with it a refreshing new voice to food writing and an honest and empowering attitude to cooking.

Nigella was prompted to write *How to Eat* out of a need to celebrate home cooking and give it the focus it deserves. She has since written nine books, as well as making several television series.

RECOMMENDED BOOKS BY NIGELLA LAWSON:

How to be a Domestic Goddess
Kitchen
Simply Nigella

What goes well with Eating?

VINTAGE MINIS

The Vintage Minis bring you the world's greatest writers on the experiences that make us human. These stylish, entertaining little books explore the whole spectrum of life – from birth to death, and everything in between. Which means there's something here for everyone, whatever your story.

Desire	Haruki Murakami
Love	Jeanette Winterson
Babies	Anne Enright
Language	Xiaolu Guo
Motherhood	Helen Simpson
Fatherhood	Karl Ove Knausgaard
Summer	Laurie Lee
Jealousy	Marcel Proust
Sisters	Louisa May Alcott
Home	Salman Rushdie
Race	Toni Morrison
Liberty	Virginia Woolf
Swimming	Roger Deakin
Work	Joseph Heller
Depression	William Styron
Drinking	John Cheever
Eating	Nigella Lawson
Psychedelics	Aldous Huxley
Calm	Tim Parks
Death	Julian Barnes